Selected Readings in Preaching

Classic Contributions from Preaching Masters

Al Fasol, Compiler

BAKER BOOK HOUSE
Grand Rapids, Michigan

The excerpt by Andrew W. Blackwood is from *The Preparation of Sermons*. Copyright renewal 1976 by Andrew W. Blackwood, Jr., Philip T. Blackwood, James R. Blackwood, and William T. Blackwood. Used by permission of Abingdon Press.

The excerpt by Halford E. Luccock is from *In the Minister's Workshop*. Copyright renewal 1972 by Mary W. Luccock. Used by permission of Abingdon Press.

The excerpt by Joseph Fort Newton is from *The New Preaching*. Copyright renewal 1957 by Joseph E. Newton and Josephine Newton Hooven. Used by permission of Abingdon Press.

Preface

There are several books on homiletics that have made classic contributions to preaching. Most seminary graduates, for instance, recognize instantly that it was Phillips Brooks who defined preaching as the communication of truth by man to men. Few, however, know how to document the quote and far fewer have ever read Brooks. Most seminary graduates can recite the name of John A. Broadus's famous treatise on preaching. But few have read it. Most seminary graduates have read sermon books by Morgan and Meyer, Spurgeon and Stewart, but few have read their distinguished lectures on preaching.

It is a staggering task for a preacher to read even some of the various books, commentaries, and journals that would be useful to him. In fact, it is discouraging to think of reading all of the good books on preaching alone, much less the other theological disciplines that deserve his attention. It is also too much of a sacrifice not to have some contact with great preachers who have written on homiletics.

Selected Readings in Preaching is a compilation of the observations of great preachers and homileticians of the past. The excerpts were selected first for their significance to the modern preacher and secondly for the variety they offer. It is hoped that these selections will inspire the preacher to read entire volumes on homiletics and to grow in his own preaching.

CONTENTS

PART ONE
The Nature of Preaching

1 Phillips Brooks. 9
   Lectures on Preaching
2 John A. Broadus. 21
   *A Treatise on the Preparation and
   Delivery of Sermons*
3 James Stuart Stewart 27
   The Preacher's World

PART TWO
Approaches to Preaching

1 G. Campbell Morgan 39
   The Essentials of a Sermon
2 Charles H. Spurgeon 53
   Sermons: Their Matter
3 Joseph Fort Newton 63
   The New Strategy
4 John A. Broadus. 67
   *A Treatise on the Preparation and Delivery
   of Sermons*

5 Charles H. Spurgeon 71
            On the Choice of a Text

6 F. B. Meyer 81
            Expository Preaching—What It Is

7 Halford E. Luccock 89
            An Art Is a Band of Music

PART THREE
Essential Qualities for Effective Preaching

1 James Stuart Stewart 97
            The Preacher's Technique

2 Joseph Parker. 101
            Earnestness

3 John Henry Jowett 111
            The Preacher in His Study

4 Andrew Blackwood 119
            The Marks of Effective Style

PART ONE
The Nature of Preaching

1
Phillips Brooks
1835-1893

One of the most concise definitions of preaching was given by Phillips Brooks: "Preaching is the communication of truth by man to men. It has in it two essential elements, truth and personality. Neither of these can it spare and still be preaching." Brooks offered this definition during his delivery of the 1877 Lyman Beecher Lectures on Preaching at Yale. The lectures were subsequently published as **Lectures on Preaching.**

Brooks was a tall, heavily built man who possessed a warm spirit. The aim of his preaching was to uplift people by showing them how to relate to God. Brooks tried to indicate how the eternal truths of God's Word related to man.

Brooks was an Episcopalian who served churches in Philadelphia and Boston. His popularity as a preacher was at its zenith from 1869 to 1891 when he served as Rector of Trinity Church in Boston.

The following excerpt was the first lecture in **Lectures on Preaching.** * *It offered a general approach to preaching and set the foundation for the five lectures which followed.*

——— —— ———

What, then, is preaching, of which we are to speak? It is not hard to find a definition. Preaching is the communication of truth by

* Phillips Brooks, *Lectures on Preaching* (1914; reprint ed., Grand Rapids: Baker Book House, 1969), pp. 5-8, 14-28.

man to men. It has in it two essential elements, truth and personality. Neither of those can it spare and still be preaching. The truest truth, the most authoritative statement of God's will, communicated in any other way than through the personality of brother man to men is not preached truth. Suppose it written on the sky, suppose it embodied in a book which has been so long held in reverence as the direct utterance of God that the vivid personality of the men who wrote its pages has well-nigh faded out of it; in neither of these cases is there any preaching. And on the other hand, if men speak to other men that which they do not claim for truth, if they use their powers of persuasion or of entertainment to make other men listen to their speculations, or do their will, or applaud their cleverness, that is not preaching either. The first lacks personality. The second lacks truth. And preaching is the bringing of truth through personality. It must have both elements. It is in the different proportion in which the two are mingled that the difference between two great classes of sermons and preaching lies. It is in the defect of one or the other element that every sermon and preacher falls short of the perfect standard. It is in the absence of one or the other element that a discourse ceases to be a sermon, and a man ceases to be a preacher altogether.

If we go back to the beginning of the Christian ministry we can see how distinctly and deliberately Jesus chose this method of extending the knowledge of Himself throughout the world. Other methods no doubt were open to Him, but He deliberately selected this. He taught His truth to a few men and then He said, "Now go and tell that truth to other men." Both elements were there, in John the Baptist who prepared the way for Him, in the seventy whom He sent out before His face, and in the little company who started from the chamber of the Pentecost to proclaim the new salvation to the world. If He gave them the power of working miracles, the miracles themselves were not the final purpose for which He gave it. The power of miracle was, as it were, a divine fire pervading the Apostle's being and opening his individuality on either side; making it more open God-wards by the sense of awful privilege, making it more open man-wards by the impressiveness and the helpfulness with which it was clothed. Everything that was peculiar in Christ's treatment of those men was merely part of the process by which the Master prepared their personality to be a fit medium for the communication of His Word. When His treatment of them was complete, they stood fused like glass, and able to take God's truth in perfectly on one side and send it out perfectly on the other side of their transparent natures.

This was the method by which Christ chose that His Gospel should be spread through the world. It was a method that might have been applied to the dissemination of any truth, but we can see why it was especially adapted to the truth of Christianity. For that truth is preeminently personal. However the Gospel may be capable of statement in dogmatic form, its truest statement we know is not in dogma but in personal life. Christianity is Christ; and we can easily understand how a truth which is of such peculiar character that a person can stand forth and say of it, "I am the Truth," must always be best conveyed through, must indeed be almost incapable of being perfectly conveyed except through personality. And so some form of preaching must be essential to the prevalence and spread of the knowledge of Christ among men. There seems to be some such meaning as this in the words of Jesus when He said to His disciples, "As My Father has sent Me into the world, even so have I sent you into the world." It was the continuation, out to the minutest ramifications of the new system of influence, of that personal method which the Incarnation itself had involved.

If this be true, then, it establishes the first of all principles concerning the ministry and preparation for the ministry. Truth through Personality is our description of real preaching. The truth must come really through the person, not merely over his lips, not merely into his understanding and out through his pen. It must come through his character, his affections, his whole intellectual and moral being. It must come genuinely through him. I think that, granting equal intelligence and study, here is the great difference which we feel between two preachers of the Word. The Gospel has come *over* one of them and reaches us tinged and flavored with his superficial characteristics, belittled with his littleness. The Gospel has come *through* the other, and we receive it impressed and winged with all the earnestness and strength that there is in him. In the first case the man has been but a printing machine or a trumpet. In the other case he has been a true man and a real messenger of God. We know how the views which theologians have taken of the agency of the Bible writers in their work differ just here. There have been those who would make them mere passive instruments. The thought of our own time has more and more tended to consider them the active messengers of the Word of God. This is the higher thought of inspiration. And this is the only true thought of the Christian preachership. . . .

Let us look now for a few moments at these two elements of preaching—Truth and Personality; the one universal and invariable, the other special and always different. There are a few suggestions that I should like to make to you about each.

And first with regard to the Truth. It is strange how impossible it is to separate it and consider it wholly by itself. The personalness will cling to it. There are two aspects of the minister's work, which we are constantly meeting in the New Testament. They are really embodied in two words, one of which is "message," and the other is "witness." "This is the message which we have heard of Him and declare unto you," says St. John in his first Epistle. "We are His witnesses of these things," says St. Peter before the Council at Jerusalem. In these two words together, I think, we have the fundamental conception of the matter of all Christian preaching. It is to be a message given to us for transmission, but yet a message which we cannot transmit until it has entered into our own experience, and we can give our own testimony of its spiritual power. The minister who keeps the word "message" always written before him, as he prepares his sermon in his study, or utters it from his pulpit, is saved from the tendency to wanton and wild speculation, and from the mere passion of originality. He who never forgets that word "witness," is saved from the unreality of repeating by rote mere forms of statement which he has learned as orthodox, but never realized as true. If you and I can always carry this double consciousness, that we are messengers, and that we are witnesses, we shall have in our preaching all the authority and independence of assured truth, and yet all the appeal and convincingness of personal belief. It will not be we that speak, but the spirit of our Father that speaketh in us, and yet our sonship shall give the Father's voice its utterance and interpretation to His other children.

I think that nothing is more needed to correct the peculiar vices of preaching which belong to our time, than a new prevalence among preachers of this first conception of the truth which they have to tell as a message. I am sure that one great source of the weakness of the pulpit is the feeling among the people that these men who stand up before them every Sunday have been making up trains of thought, and thinking how they should "treat their subject," as the phrase runs. There is the first ground of the vicious habit that our congregations have of talking about the preacher more than they think about the truth. The minstrel who sings before you to show his skill, will be praised for his wit, and rhymes, and voice. But the courier who hurries in, breathless, to bring you a message, will be forgotten in the message that he brings. Among the many sermons I have heard, I always remember one, for the wonderful way in which it was pervaded by this quality. It was a sermon by Mr. George Macdonald, the English author, who was in this country a few years ago; and it had many of the good and bad characteristics of his interesting style. It had his brave and manly honesty, and his tendency to sentimentality. But over and through it all it had this quality: it was a message from God to these people by him. The man struggled with language as a child struggles with his imperfectly mastered tongue, that will not tell the errand as he received it, and has it in his mind. As I listened, I seemed to see how weak in contrast was the way in which other preachers had amused me and challenged my admiration for the working of their minds. Here was a gospel. Here were real tidings. And you listened and forgot the preacher.

Whatever else you count yourself in the ministry, never lose this fundamental idea of yourself as a messenger. As to the way in which one shall best keep that idea, it would not be hard to state; but it would involve the whole story of the Christian life. Here is the primary necessity that the Christian preacher should be a Christian first, that he should be deeply cognizant of God's authority, and of the absoluteness of Christ's truth. That was one of the first principles which I ventured to assume as I began my lecture. But without entering so wide a field, let me say one thing about this conception of preaching as the telling of a message which constantly impresses me. I think that it would give to our preaching just the quality which it appears to me to most lack now. That quality is breadth. I do not mean liberality of thought, nor tolerance of opinion, nor anything of that kind. I mean largeness of movement, the great utterance of great truths, the great enforcement of great duties, as distinct from the minute, and subtle, and ingenious treatment of little topics, side issues of the soul's life, bits of anatomy, the bric-a-brac of theology. Take up, some Saturday, the list of subjects on which the ministers of a great city are to preach the next day. See how many of them seem to have searched in strange corners of the Bible for their topics, how small and fantastic is the bit of truth which their hearers are to have set before them. Then turn to Barrow, or Tillotson, or Bushnell—"Of being imitators of Christ"; "That God is the only happiness of man"; "Every man's life a plan of God." There is a painting of ivory miniatures, and there is a painting of great frescoes. One kind of art is suited to one kind of subject, and another to another. I suppose that all preachers pass through some fantastic period when a strange text fascinates them; when they like to find what can be said for an hour on some little topic on which most men could only talk two minutes; when they are eager for subtlety more than force, and for originality more than truth. But as a preacher grows more full of the conception of the sermon as a message, he gets clear of those brambles. He comes out on to open ground. His work grows freer, and bolder, and broader. He loves the simplest texts, and the great truths which run like rivers through all life. God's sovereignty, Christ's redemption, man's hope in the Spirit, the privilege of duty, the love of man in the Saviour, make the strong music which his soul tries to catch.

And then another result of this conception of preaching as the telling of a message is that it puts us into right relations with all historic Christianity. The message never can be told as if we were the first to tell it. It is the same message which the Church has told in all the ages. He who tells it to-day is backed by all the multitude who have told it in the past. He is companied by all those who are telling it now. The message is his witness; but a part of the assurance with which he has received it, comes from the fact of its being the identical message which has come down from the beginning. Men find on both sides how difficult it is to preserve the true poise and proportion between the corporate and the individual conceptions of the Christian life. But all will own to-day the need of both. The identity of the Church in all times consists in the identity of the message which she has always had to carry from her Lord to men. All outward utterances of the perpetual identity of the Church are valuable only as they assert this real identity. There is the real meaning of the perpetuation of old ceremonies, the use of ancient liturgies, and the clinging to what seem to be apostolic types of government. The heretic in all times has been not the errorist as such, but the self-willed man, whether his judgments were right or wrong. "A man may be a heretic in the truth," says Milton. He is the man who, taking his ideas not as a message from God, but as his own discoveries, has cut himself off from the message-bearing Church of all the ages. I am sure that the more fully you come to count your preaching the telling of a message, the more valuable and real the Church will become to you, the more true will seem to you your brotherhood with all messengers of that same message in all strange dresses and in all strange tongues.

I should like to mention, with reference to the Truth which the preacher has to preach, two tendencies which I am sure that you will recognize as very characteristic of our time. One is the tendency of criticism, and the other is the tendency of mechanism. Both tendencies are bad. By the tendency of criticism I mean the

disposition that prevails everywhere to deal with things from out-
side, discussing their relations, examining their nature, and not
putting ourselves into their power. Preaching in every age follows,
to a certain extent, the changes which come to all literature and
life. The age in which we live is strangely fond of criticism. It takes
all things to pieces for the mere pleasure of examining their nature.
It studies forces, not in order to obey them, but in order to understand them. It talks about things for the pure pleasure of discussion.
Much of the poetry and prose about nature and her wonders, much
of the investigation of the country's genius and institutions, much
of the subtle analysis of human nature is of this sort. It is all good;
but it is something distinct from the cordial sympathy by which
one becomes a willing servant of any of these powers, a real lover
of nature, or a faithful citizen, or a true friend. Now it would be
strange if this critical tendency did not take possession of the
preaching of the day. And it does. The disposition to watch ideas in
their working, and to talk about their relations and their influence
on one another, simply as problems, in which the mind may find
pleasure without any real entrance of the soul into the ideas themselves, this, which is the critical tendency, invades the pulpit, and
the result is an immense amount of preaching which must be called
preaching about Christ as distinct from preaching Christ. There
are many preachers who seem to do nothing else, always discussing
Christianity as a problem instead of announcing Christianity as a
message, and proclaiming Christ as a Saviour. I do not undervalue
their discussions. But I think we ought always to feel that such discussions are not the type or ideal of preaching. They may be necessities of the time, but they are not the work which the great Apostolic preachers did, or which the true preacher will always most
desire. Definers and defenders of the faith are always needed, but it
is bad for a church when its ministers count it their true work to
define and defend the faith rather than to preach the Gospel. Beware of the tendency to preach about Christianity, and try to
preach Christ. To discuss the relations of Christianity and Science,
Christianity and Society, Christianity and Politics, is good. To set
Christ forth to men so that they shall know Him, and in gratitude
and love become His, that is far better. It is good to be a Herschel
who describes the sun; but it is better to be a Prometheus who
brings the sun's fire to the earth.

I called the other tendency the tendency of mechanism. It is the
disposition of the preacher to forget that the Gospel of Christ is
primarily addressed to individuals, and that its ultimate purpose is

the salvation of multitudes of men. Between the time when it first speaks to a man's soul, and the time when that man's soul is gathered into heaven, with the whole host of the redeemed, the Gospel uses a great many machineries which are more or less impersonal. The Church, with all its instrumentalities, comes in. The preacher works by them. But if the preacher ever for a moment counts them the purpose of his working, if he takes his eyes off the single soul as the prize he is to win, he falls from his highest function and loses his best power. All successful preaching, I more and more believe, talks to individuals. The Church is for the soul. I am not thinking of the fault or danger of any one body of Christians alone when I say this, not of my own or any other. The tendency to work for the means instead of for the end is everywhere. And, my friends, learn this at the beginning of your ministry, that just as surely as you think that any kind of fault or danger belongs wholly to another system than your own, and that you are not exposed to it, just so surely you will reproduce that fault or danger in some form in your own life. This surely is a good rule: whenever you see a fault in any other man, or any other church, look for it in yourself and in your own church. Where is the church which is not liable to value its machineries above its purposes, whose ministers are not tempted to preach for the denomination and its precious peculiarities, instead of for men and for their precious souls? Let your preaching be to individuals, and to the Church always as living for and made up of individuals.

Of the second element in preaching, namely, the preacher's personality, there will be a great deal to say, especially in the next lecture. But there are two or three fundamental things which I wish to say to-day.

The first is this, that the principle of personality once admitted involves the individuality of every preacher. The same considerations which make it good that the Gospel should not be written on the sky, or committed merely to an almost impersonal book, make it also most desirable that every preacher should utter the truth in his own way, and according to his own nature. It must come not only through man but through men. If you monotonize men you lose their human power to a large degree. If you could make all men think alike it would be very much as if no man thought at all, as when the whole earth moves together with all that is upon it, everything seems still. Now the deep sense of the solemnity of the minister's work has often a tendency to repress the free individuality of the preacher and his tolerance of other preachers' individualities. His own way of doing his work is with him a matter of conscience, not of taste, and the conscience when it is thoroughly awake is more intolerant than the taste is. Or, working just the other way, his conscience tells him that it is not for him to let his personal peculiarities intrude in such a solemn work, and so he tries to bind himself to the ways of working which the most successful preachers of the Word have followed. I have seen both these kinds of ministers: those whose consciences made them obstinate, and those whose consciences made them pliable; those whose consciences hardened them to steel or softened them to wax. However it comes about, there is an unmistakable tendency to the repression of the individuality of the preacher. It is seen in little things: in the uniform which preachers wear and the disposition to a uniformity of language. It is seen in great things: in the disposition which all ages have witnessed to draw a line of orthodoxy inside the lines of truth. Wisely and soberly let us set ourselves against this influence. The God who sent men to preach the Gospel of His Son in their humanity, sent each man distinctively to preach it in his humanity. Be yourself by all means, but let that good result come not by cultivating merely superficial peculiarities and oddities. Let it be by winning a true self full of your own faith and your own love. The deep originality is noble, but the surface originality is miserable. It is so easy to be a John the Baptist, as far as the desert and camel's hair and locusts and wild honey go. But the devoted heart to speak from, and the fiery words to speak, are other things.

Again, we never can forget in thinking of the preacher's personality that he is one who lives in constant familiarity with thoughts and words which to other men are occasional and rare, and which preserve their sacredness mainly by their rarity. That fact must always come in when we try to estimate the influences of a preacher's life. What will the power of that fact be? I am sure that often it weakens the minister. I am sure that many men who, if they came to preach once in a great while in the midst of other occupations, would preach with reality and fire, are deadened to their sacred work by their constant intercourse with sacred things. Their constant dealing with the truth makes them less powerful to bear the truth to others, as a pipe through which the water always flows collects its sediment, and is less fit to let more water through. And besides this, it ministers to self-deception and to an exaggeration or distortion of our own history. The man who constantly talks of certain experiences, and urges other men to enter into them, must come in time, by very force of describing those experiences, to

think that he has undergone them. You beg men to repent, and you
grow so familiar with the whole theory of repentance that it is hard
for you to know that you yourself have not repented. You exhort to
patience till you have no eyes or ears for your own impatience. It is
the way in which the man who starts the trains at the railroad sta-
tion must come in time to feel as if he himself had been to all the
towns along the road whose names he has always been shouting in
the passengers' ears, and to which he has for years sold them their
tickets, when perhaps he has not left his own little way-station all
the time. I know that all this is so, and yet certainly the fault is in
the man, not in the truth. The remedy certainly is not to make the
truth less familiar. There is a truer relation to preaching, in which
the constancy of it shall help instead of harming the reality and
earnestness with which you do it. The more that you urge other
people to holiness the more intense may be the hungering and
thirsting after holiness in your own heart. Familiarity does not
breed contempt except of contemptible things or in contemptible
people. The adage, that no man is a hero to his *valet de chambre*, is
sufficiently answered by saying that it is only to a *valet de chambre*
that a truly great man is unheroic. You must get the impulse, the
delight, and the growing sacredness of your life out of your familiar work. You are lost as a preacher if its familiarity deadens and
encrusts, instead of vitalizing and opening your powers. And it will
all depend upon whether you do your work for your Master and
His people or for yourself. The last kind of labor slowly kills, the
first gives life more and more.

The real preparation of the preacher's personality for its trans-
missive work comes by the opening of his life on both sides,
towards the truth of God and towards the needs of man. To apprehend in all their intensity the wants and woes of men, to see the
problems and dangers of this life, then to know all through us that
nothing but Christ and His Redemption can thoroughly satisfy
these wants, that is what makes a man a preacher. Alas for him
who is only open on the man-ward side, who only knows how miserable and wicked man is, but has no power of God to bring to
him. He lays a kind but helpless hand upon the wound. He tries to
relieve it with his sympathy and his philosophy. He is the source of
all he says. There is no God behind him. He is no preacher. The
preacher's instinct is that which feels instantly how Christ and human need belong together, neither thinks Christ too far off for the
need, nor the need too insignificant for Christ. Never be afraid to
bring the transcendent mysteries of our faith, Christ's life and

death and resurrection, to the help of the humblest and commonest of human wants. There is a sort of preaching which keeps them for the great emergencies, and soothes the common sorrows and rebukes the common sins with lower considerations of economy. Such preaching fails. It neither appeals to the lower nor to the higher perceptions of mankind. It is useful neither as a law nor as a gospel. It is like a river that is frozen too hard to be navigable but not hard enough to bear. Never fear, as you preach, to bring the sublimest motive to the smallest duty, and the most infinite comfort to the smallest trouble. They will prove that they belong there if only the duty and trouble are real and you have read them thoroughly aright.

These are the elements of preaching, then—Truth and Personality. The truth is in itself a fixed and stable element; the personality is a varying and growing element. In the union of the two we have the provision for the combination of identity with variety, of stability with growth, in the preaching of the Gospel.

2
John A. Broadus
1827-1895

*One of the oldest and most influential books on preaching is **A Treatise on the Preparation and Delivery of Sermons**, written in 1870 by John A. Broadus. The book has been revised by three editors. Many other authors of books on preaching have consulted Broadus as they wrote their books.*

Broadus's commentary on Matthew in the American Commentary Series is considered a classic by many New Testament scholars. He served as pastor of several churches in Virginia and South Carolina before becoming president of the Baptist Seminary, Greenville, South Carolina. Broadus became president of Southern Baptist Seminary in Louisville, Kentucky, in 1889, the same year in which he delivered the Lyman Beecher Lectures on Preaching at Yale.

*The following excerpt is from the introduction to **A Treatise on the Preparation and Delivery of Sermons**.* * *The excerpt conveys Broadus's views on the nature of preaching.*

Preaching is characteristic of Christianity. No false religion has ever provided for the regular and frequent assembling of the masses of men, to hear religious instruction and exhortation. Judaism had something like it in the prophets, and afterwards in

---

* John A. Broadus, *A Treatise on the Preparation and Delivery of Sermons* (New York: Hodder and Stoughton, 1898), pp. 1-7.

the readers and speakers of the synagogue; but Judaism was a true religion, designed to be developed into Christianity.

It is true that some heathen religious teachers, seeing the power of preaching, have at times tried to imitate Christianity in this respect. Thus the Roman emperor Julian, commonly called the Apostate, directed the pagan philosophers to preach every week as the Christians did. And in modern times there are said to have been in China, Japan, and India instances of the adoption of something like preaching. But so far as is known preaching remains, both in origin and history, a peculiarly Christian institution.

The great appointed means of spreading the good tidings of salvation through Christ is preaching—words spoken whether to the individual, or to the assembly. And this, nothing can supersede. *Printing* has become a mighty agency for good and for evil; and Christians should employ it, with the utmost diligence and in every possible way, for the spread of truth. But printing can never take the place of the living word. When a man who is apt in teaching, whose soul is on fire with the truth which he trusts has saved him and hopes will save others, speaks to his fellowmen, face to face, eye to eye, and electric sympathies flash to and fro between him and his hearers, till they lift each other up, higher and higher, into the intensest thought, and the most impassioned emotion—higher and yet higher, till they are borne as on chariots of fire above the world,—there is power to move men, to influence character, life, destiny, such as no printed page can ever possess. *Pastoral work* is of immense importance, and all preachers should be diligent in performing it. But it cannot take the place of preaching, nor fully compensate for lack of power in the pulpit. The two help each other, and neither of them is able, unless supported by the other, to achieve the largest and most blessed results. When he who preaches is the sympathizing pastor, the trusted counsellor, the kindly and honored friend of young and old, of rich and poor, then "truths divine come mended from his lips," and the door to men's hearts, by the magical power of sympathy, will fly open at his word. But on the other hand, when he who visits is the preacher, whose thorough knowledge of Scripture and elevated views of life, whose able and impassioned discourses have carried conviction and commanded admiration, and melted into one the hearts of the multitude, who is accustomed to stand before them as the ambassador of God, and is associated in their minds with the authority and the sacredness of God's Word—when *he* comes to speak with the suffering, the sorrowing, the tempted, his visit has a meaning and a power of which otherwise it must be destitute. If a minister feels himself specially drawn towards either of these departments of effort, let him also constrain himself to diligence in the other.

Religious *ceremonies* may be instructive and impressive. The older dispensation made much use of these, as we employ pictures in teaching children. Even Christianity, which has the minimum of ceremony, illustrates its fundamental facts, and often makes deep religious impressions, by its two simple but expressive ordinances. But these are merely pictures to illustrate, merely helps to that great work of teaching and convincing, of winning and holding men, which preaching, made mighty by God's Spirit, has to perform.

It follows that preaching must always be a necessity, and good preaching a mighty power. In every age of Christianity, since John the Baptist drew crowds into the desert, there has been no great religious movement, no restoration of Scripture truth, and reanimation of genuine piety, without new power in preaching, both as cause and as effect.

But alas! how difficult we find it to preach *well*. How small a proportion of the sermons heard weekly throughout the world are really good. The dilettanti men of letters who every now and then fill the periodicals with sneers at preaching, no doubt judge most unkindly and unjustly, for they purposely compare ordinary examples of preaching with the finest specimens of literature, and they forget their own utter lack, in the one case, of that sympathetic appreciation without which all literary and artistic judgment is necessarily at fault; but we who love preaching and who try to preach are better aware than they are, of the deficiencies which mar our efforts, and the difficulties which attend our work. A venerable and eminently useful minister once remarked, as he rose from the couch on which he had been resting, "Well, I must get ready to preach to-night. But I can't preach—I never did preach—O, I never *heard anybody preach.*"

And yet in this work of ours, so awful and so attractive, so difficult and solemnly responsible and yet so blessed, we ought to aspire after the highest excellence. If in other varieties of public speaking, then most of all in this, may we adopt Cicero's words with reference to the young orator, "I will not only exhort, but will even beseech him, to labor."

What is good preaching? Or, more generally, what is eloquence? This is not a merely speculative inquiry, for our fundamental views on the subject will influence, to a greater extent than we may be aware, our practical efforts. Without reviewing the copious discussions of the question, the following statement may be offered: Eloquence is so speaking as not merely to convince the judgment, kindle the imagination, and move the feelings, but to give a powerful impulse to the will. All of these are necessary elements of eloquence, but that which is most characteristic is the last. There may be instruction and conviction without eloquence. The fancy may be charmed, as by a poem or novel, when you would not think of calling it eloquence. The feelings may be deeply stirred by a pathetic tale or a harrowing description, but no corresponding action being proposed, we do not speak of it as eloquence. On the other hand, it is not strictly correct to say that "eloquence is so speaking as to carry your point;" for there may be an invincible prejudice, or other insuperable obstacle, as, for example, a preacher may be truly eloquent, without actually inducing his hearers to repent. There must be a *powerful impulse* upon the will; the hearers must feel smitten, stirred, moved to, or at least moved towards, some action or determination to act. Words that by carrying conviction, kindling imagination, and arousing emotion, produce such an effect as this upon the will, are rightly called eloquent words. Augustine says, *Veritas pateat, veritas placeat, veritas moveat*, "Make the truth plain, make it pleasing, make it moving."

Eloquence, then, is a practical thing. Unless it aims at real and practical results, it is spurious. Daniel O'Connell, the famous Irish patriot and lawyer, is credited with the saying, "A good speech is a good thing, but the verdict is *the* thing." Mere holiday eloquence does not deserve the name. And the preacher who kindles the fancy of his hearers merely for their delectation, who stirs their passions merely to give them the luxury of emotion, is not eloquent. There is too much preaching of just this sort. Besides vain pretenders who care only to please, there are good men, who, if they can say very handsome things, and can make the people *feel*, imagine that they are preaching well, without inquiring *why* the people feel, and to what truly religious ends the feeling is directed. It is a shame to see what vapid and worthless stuff is often called eloquence, in newspaper puffs, and in the talk of the half-educated younglings returning from the church.

Eloquence is a serious thing. You cannot say that a discourse, or a paragraph, is very amusing and very eloquent. The speaker who is to deserve this high name must have moral earnestness. He may sometimes indulge, where it is appropriate, in the light play of delicate humor, or give forth sparks of wit, but these must be entirely incidental, and subordinate to a thorough seriousness and earnestness. Theremin, in his useful little treatise, "Eloquence a Virtue," insists that eloquence belongs to the ethical sciences, the character and spirit of the speaker being the main thing. The theory is an exaggeration, but contains an important element of truth, as Quintilian already had partly observed.

"What is the true ground of eloquence," says Vinet, "if it is not commonplace? When eloquence is combined with high philosophical considerations, as in many modern examples, we are at first tempted to attribute to philosophy the impression we receive from it; but eloquence is something more popular; it is the power of making the primitive chords of the soul (its purely human elements) vibrate within us—it is in this, and nothing else, that we acknowledge the orator." It is impossible to be eloquent on any subject, save by associating it with such ideas as that of mother, child, friends, home, country, heaven, and the like; all of them familiar, and, in themselves, commonplace. The speaker's task is, by his grouping, illustration, etc., and by his own contagious emotion, to invest these familiar ideas with fresh interest, so that they may reassert their power over the hearts of his hearers. He who runs after material of discourse that shall be absolutely new, may get credit for originality, and be amply admired, but he will not exert the living power which belongs to eloquence. The *preacher* can be really eloquent only when he speaks of those vital gospel truths which have necessarily become familiar. A just rhetoric, if there were no higher consideration, would require that a preacher shall preach the gospel—shall hold on to the old truths, and labor to clothe them with new interest and power.

3

James Stuart Stewart

1896-

*A native of Scotland, James Stuart Stewart served as a pastor, professor, and lecturer prior to his formal retirement in 1966. His preaching included both evangelistic and ethical emphases. Several books of Stewart's sermons have been published, but his most significant contribution to preaching is **Heralds of God**. The book contains the Warrack Lectures delivered by Stewart at the University of Edinburgh. The excerpt which follows is from the first lecture which Stewart titled "The Preacher's World."* It deals with Stewart's philosophy of preaching. The other lecture titles are: "The Preacher's Theme," "The Preacher's Study," "The Preacher's Technique," and "The Preacher's Inner Life." Part III of this book includes a portion of Stewart's lecture on "The Preacher's Technique," which deals with the use of clear language.*

——— ——— ———

It is quite impossible to preach Christ faithfully without saying many things which will sting the natural heart of man into opposition and rebellion. You will have to declare, for example, that to imagine one can receive God's forgiveness while refusing oneself to be forgiving to others is sophistry and deceit: a hard saying that for many. Or take the doctrine of the divine Fatherhood. There are still those who accept that doctrine and sun themselves in its warm and comforting glow, but resent being confronted with its dis-

* James S. Stewart, *Heralds of God* (1946; reprint ed., Grand Rapids: Baker Book House, 1972), pp. 30-44, 47-48.

concerting and inexorable implications in the realm of practical brotherhood and social ethics. "Give us the simple Gospel," they cry: escapism rationalizing itself again. Take even the missionary challenge and the conception of a universal Church. We believe that, just as no man is truly awake to-day who has not developed a supra-national horizon to his thinking, so no Church is anything more than a pathetic pietistic backwater unless it is first and fundamentally and all the time a world missionary Church. But there are stubborn strongholds into which that truth has yet to penetrate—minds which for one reason or another, persistently regard the missionary enterprise as the province of a few enthusiasts, a side-show, an extra: not realizing that here is something which every professing Christian must espouse with all his heart and soul, or else surrender his right to march beneath the banners of Christ. It is your task as preachers to summon men to share with Jesus in the great crusade which began at Calvary and Pentecost, and shall never cease until the whole earth is filled with the glory of the Lord; and where the narrower view prevails, you must at all costs disturb its contentment and bid it reflect what it will feel like for any disciple to stand before Christ at last and say, "The world mission of Your religion had no help from me!"

Therefore resist all temptations to dilute your Gospel. Your task is not to send people away from church, saying, "That was a lovely sermon" or "What an eloquent appeal!" The one question is: Did they, or did they not, meet God to-day? There will always be some who have no desire for that, some who rather than be confronted with the living Christ would actually prefer what G. K. Chesterton described as "one solid and polished cataract of platitudes flowing for ever and ever." But when St. Peter finished his first great sermon in Jerusalem, reported in the Book of Acts, I do not read that "when they heard this, they were intrigued by his eloquence" or "politely interested in his literary allusions," or "critical of his logic and his accent," or "bored and impassive and contemptuous"; what I do read is: "When they heard this, they were pierced to the heart." The heart of man has a whole armour of escapist devices to hold off the danger when reality comes too near. But I would remind you that Peter's theme that day—Jesus crucified and risen—is your basic message still: still as dynamic, as "mighty through God to the pulling down of strongholds," as moving and heart-piercing, as when men heard it preached in Jerusalem long ago.

There is, however, another side to the matter. Just as we noted how profoundly the modern mind is dominated by the tension between disillusionment and hope, so now we have to observe that over against the escapist attitude, countering it and setting up a further tension, there exists a strange passion for reality. Illogical? Undoubtedly. But there is the fact governing the relationship of multitudes at this moment to the religion of Christ—what repels, attracts; what disturbs and disconcerts, haunts and convinces. In the very moment of the headlong flight from reality, the drive towards reality makes itself felt; and "Depart from me, for I am a sinful man" becomes "Nearer, my God, to Thee!"

It is one of the mightiest safeguards of a man's ministry—to be aware of that hungry demand for reality breaking inarticulately from the hearts of those to whom he ministers. For that cry puts everything shoddy, second-hand, or artificial utterly to shame.

You do not need to be eloquent, or clever, or sensational, or skilled in dialectic; you *must* be real. To fail there is to fail abysmally and tragically. It is to damage incalculably the cause you represent.

Anything savouring of unreality in the pulpit is double offence. Let me urge upon you two considerations.

On the one hand, you will be preaching to people who have been grappling all the week with stern realities. Behind a congregation assembling for worship there are stories of heavy anxiety and fierce temptation, of loneliness and heroism, of overwork and lack of work, of physical strain and mental wear and tear. We wrong them and we mock their struggles if we preach our Gospel in abstraction from the hard facts of their experience. It is not only that they can detect at once the hollowness of such a performance, though that is true; there is also this—that to offer pedantic theorizings and academic irrelevances to souls wrestling in the dark is to sin against the Lord who died for them and yearns for their redeeming.

But there is a further indictment of unreality in preaching. This is rooted not so much in the hard problems men and women are facing—what Whittier called this "maddening maze of things"—as in the very nature of the Christian faith itself. The Gospel is quite shattering in its realism. It shirks nothing. It never seeks to gloss over the dark perplexities of fate, frustration, sin and death, or to gild unpalatable facts with a coating of pious verbiage or facile consolation. It never side-tracks uncomfortable questions with some naive and cheerful cliche about providence or progress. It gazes open-eyed at the most menacing and savage circumstance that life can show. It is utterly courageous. Its strength is the complete absence of utopian illusions. It thrusts Golgotha upon men's vision and bids them look at that. The very last charge which can be brought against the Gospel is that of sentimentality, of blinking the facts. It is devastating in its veracity, and its realism is a consuming fire.

This is the message with which we are charged. How grievous the fault if in our hands it becomes tainted with unreality!

Of course, this is an issue which concerns the whole Church, and not only the individual minister. Nothing so gravely compromises the Christian witness as the suspicion that organized religion is failing to practice what it preaches. There are at least three directions in which the Church to-day is having to meet and to answer the challenge of the craving for reality. The first relates to worship. Do our forms of worship convey at every point the ringing note of entire sincerity and truth? The second has to do with the social implications of the Gospel. Has it not happened all too frequently that men of generous and noble nature, tormented by the spectacle of the wrongs of society and the sufferings of humanity, and of fire to help their brethren "bound in affliction and iron," have cried out against what seemed to them the appalling torpor and inaction of the Church, dragging its slow ponderous length along, with leisurely, lumbering organization, and have flung away from it in impatience and despair? The third challenge concerns Christian unity. Is it legitimate, is it convincing, for a Church to summon men to brotherhood and solidarity, while its own ruinous divisions are manifest to all? Is it real—in a day when the thrust and pressure of anti-Christian forces ought to be driving all believers to close their ranks and march together, in a day moreover when the reaction from the hyper-individualism of a bygone age is leading the younger generation to new experiments in the realm of community—is it real to maintain and perpetuate the partisan loyalties which disrupt true fellowship and drive Christians asunder? "Physician, heal thyself!"

In these ways, then, the demand for reality impinges upon the witness of the Church at large. But what mainly concerns us here is the more personal issue. If you are wise you will register a vow, at the very outset of your ministry, to make reality your constant quest. In the fine language of Scripture, "Her merchandise is better than silver, and the gain thereof than fine gold. She is more precious than rubies: and all the things thou canst desire are not to be compared unto her." Richard Baxter, who after three hundred years is still so sure a guide, has some plain-spoken words on this matter. "It is a lamentable case, that in a message from the God of heaven, of everlasting consequences to the souls of men, we should behave ourselves so weakly, so unhandsomely, so imprudently, or so slightly, that the whole business should miscarry in our hands, and God be dishonoured, and His work disgraced, and sinners rather hardened than converted." By way of contrast, take this significant account of the effect produced by a great nineteenth-century preacher on two of the most acute and discriminating minds of his day. "We have just been to hear Spurgeon," wrote Principal Tulloch, describing a visit paid by Professor Ferrier the metaphysician and himself to the Surrey Gardens Music Hall one Sunday morning in 1858, "and have been both so much impressed that I wish to give you my impressions while they are fresh. As we came out we both confessed, 'There is no doubt about *that*,' and I was struck with Ferrier's remarkable expression, 'I feel it would do me good to hear the like of that; it sat so close to reality.' The sermon is about the most real thing I have come in contact with for a long time." That focuses the basic element of the true preacher's power. "It sat so close to reality." *O si sic omnes!*

To make this quite concrete, let me urge upon you the following maxims.

Be real in worship. If you are to lead others in worship, you must be truly sharing in the act of worship yourself. No doubt this sounds self-evident; yet it does need to be emphasized. I mean, for instance, that you are not to occupy the time of hymn-singing conning the Scripture lessons or fidgeting with a sheaf of intimations or moving restlessly about the pulpit or scanning the congregation for absentees. It is unnatural to bid your people lift up their hearts to the Lord and then fail to join your voice with theirs in the common act of praise. Moreover, it is by realizing the attitude of worship in your own spirit that you will best find deliverance from awkward mannerisms, from the blight of self-consciousness, and even from that deadly menace, the "pulpit voice," than which nothing is more infallibly destructive of the atmosphere of reality. And if you will remember that the sermon itself should be an act of worship, a sacramental showing forth of Christ, will not that save you from a multitude of pitfalls? You are not likely to become pompous or pretentious or pontifical if you are truly seeing Jesus and helping others to see Him. You will not scold or rate or lecture when God's Word is on your mouth. "Have you ever heard me preach?" Coleridge asked Charles Lamb one day; to which Lamb replied, "I never heard you do anything else." But it is a different preaching which creates the hush that tells when Christ is in the midst. There is nothing like worship, when it is real, for destroying every shred and atom of a man's self-importance. A minister of God who carries a sense of his importance about with him, even into the pulpit, is a dreadful and pathetic sight: but who will say it is unknown?

> There are a sort of men whose visages
> Do cream and mantle like a standing pond,
> And do a wilful stillness entertain,
> With purpose to be dress'd in an opinion
> Of wisdom, gravity, profound conceit;
> As who should say, "I am Sir Oracle,
> And when I ope my lips let no dog bark!"

Not that the corrective of a stiff and ostentatious formality is to be a slovenly and casual informality! "Some people imagine," declared the late Bernard Manning of Cambridge, "that informality in the pulpit in itself induces a belief in their sincerity or genius. It induces only a belief in their bad taste, and makes us want to get under the seats. Do not behave with a triviality, a casualness, a haphazardness, as if not merely God were absent, but as if all decent people were absent too." There is one thing, and one thing only, which can rescue the preacher from the immense besetting dangers of his position, and that is to have his own spirit bathed in the atmosphere of worship, awed and subdued and thrilled that Christ should come so near. In the words of a great tribute once paid to John Brown of Haddington by no less a critic than David Hume, "That's the man for me, he means what he says: he speaks as if Jesus was at his elbow."

Be real in language. Shun everything stilted, grandiose, insipid, or pedantic. Do not be like the learned preacher who in the course of a sermon in a village church remarked, "Perhaps some of you at this point are suspecting me of Eutychianism." In your business of bringing the Christian religion decisively to bear upon the needs and problems of a twentieth-century congregation, the language of Nicaea, or even of the Westminster Divines, may be a hindrance rather than a help. It is sheer slackness to fling at your people great slabs of religious phraseology derived from a bygone age, and leave them the task of retranslation into terms of their own experience: that is your task, not theirs. Beware lest with facile platitudes and prosy commonplaces you cheapen the glorious Gospel of the blessed God. Eliminate everything which does not ring true. Be wary of indulging in oratory. "If a learned brother," said Spurgeon, "fires over the heads of his congregation with a grand oration, he may trace his elocution, if he likes, to Cicero and Demosthenes, but do not let him ascribe it to the Holy Spirit." If you have a tendency towards purple passages, suppress it sternly. A generation which is suspicious and impatient of high-sounding declamatory language in Parliament and press and on the public platform is not likely to be impressed by it in the pulpit; and if you once give men the idea that you are indulging in self-concious artistry, they will hardly believe that the things of which you speak are overmastering realities. John Bunyan declares, in the Preface to *Grace Abounding*, "I could have stepped into a style much higher than this, and could have adorned all things more than here I have seemed to do." But he is quite candid about his reason for refusing such tricks of elegance and ornament: "I dare not. God did not play in tempting of me; neither did I play, when the pangs of hell caught hold upon me; wherefore I may not play in relating of them, but be plain and simple, and lay down the thing as it was." You are to be dealing in your preaching with real things: temptation, crushing grief, the fear of death, the grace of Christ. On such themes, you cannot indulge in florid writing and preciosity without seeming to deny their reality. "We talk now," exclaimed Joseph Parker, "about sermons being polished, and finished, and exquisite, with many a delicate little touch artistic. The Lord send fire upon all such abortions and burn them up, till their white ashes cannot any more be found!"

This is not to ban emotion from preaching. Any such advice would be supremely foolish. No man who realizes what is at stake—the depth of the human plight and the wonder of the divine remedy—will lack the authentic touch of passion. The preacher, said Lacordaire, is like Mount Horeb: "before God strikes him he is but a barren rock, but as soon as the divine hand has touched him, as it were with a finger, there burst forth streams that water the desert." What I would warn you against is not the genuine note of feeling that will carry your words like winged things into many a heart: it is that self-conscious straining after effect which may be legitimate in the schools of the sophists but is totally out of place at the mercy-seat of God. "Great sermons," declared Henry Ward Beecher, "are nuisances. Show-sermons are the temptation of the devil." Life and death issues are in your mouth when you preach the Gospel of Christ; and it is simply tragic trifling to make the sermon a declamatory firework show, or a garish display of the flow of rhetoric. Have you ever marvelled at the Bible's sublime economy of words? Take a story like the coming of Ruth and

Naomi. There is no striving after literary effect; the whole thing is told in short, quiet, almost staccato sentences; not a word is wasted. Yet how packed with emotion it is, how truly and profoundly moving! Or take the chapter which describes how David in the unguarded hour broke faith with his own soul and with God. Could any flamboyant eloquence of denunciation have equalled the overwhelming effect of those quiet words at the close: "But the thing that David had done displeased the Lord"? Above all, take the Passion narratives in the Gospels. How their restraint rebukes our vain embellishments! How crude and turgid those cherished purple passages begin to look in the light of the Word of God! Christ's messengers are sent forth armed with a Word able to break men's hearts and heal them. But remember—as Richard Baxter told the preachers of his day—"you cannot break men's hearts by patching up a gaudy oration." Be real in language!

Finally, I would say this: *Be real in your total attitude to the message.* There is something wrong if a man, charged with the greatest news in the world, can be listless and frigid and feckless and dull. Who is going to believe that the tidings brought by the preacher matter literally more than anything else on earth if they are presented with no sort of verve or fire or attack, and if the man himself is apathetic and uninspired, afflicted with spiritual coma, and unsaying by his attitude what he says in words? There is no prayer that ought to be more constantly on your lips than those lines of Charles Wesley, surely the most characteristic he ever wrote:

> O Thou who camest from above,
> The pure celestial fire to impart,
> Kindle a flame of sacred love
> On the mean altar of my heart.
> There let it for Thy glory burn.

Think of the news you are ordained to declare. That God has invaded history with power and great glory; that in the day of man's terrible need a second Adam has come forth to the fight and to the rescue; that in the Cross the supreme triumph of naked evil has been turned once for all to irrevocable defeat; that Christ is alive now and present through His Spirit; that through the risen Christ there has been let loose into the world a force which can transform life beyond recognition—this is the most momentous message human lips were ever charged to speak. It dwarfs all other truths into insignificance. It is electrifying in its power, shattering in its wonder. Surely it is desperately unreal to talk of themes like these in a

voice deadened by routine, or in the maddeningly offhand and impassive manner which is all too familiar. It ought not to be possible
to conduct a Church service in a way which leaves a stranger with
the impression that nothing particular is happening and that no
important business is on hand. "Went to Church to-day," wrote
Robert Louis Stevenson in his journal, "and was not greatly de-
pressed." If that is the best we can do for people, is it worth doing?
"Certainly I must confess," cried Sir Philip Sidney, "I never heard
the old song of Percy and Douglas, that I found not my heart
moved more than with a trumpet." And to you has been committed
the infinitely more heart-moving story of the Word made flesh:
"that incredible interruption," wrote G. K. Chesterton, "as a blow
that broke the very backbone of history." "It were better," he declared, "to rend our robes with a great cry against blasphemy, like
Caiaphas in the judgment, rather than to stand stupidly debating
fine shades of pantheism in the presence of so catastrophic a
claim."

What strikes you about the preachers of the New Testament is
that they had been swept off their feet and carried away by the
glory of the great revelation. They went to men who had sinned
disastrously, and they cried, "Listen! We can tell you of reconcilia-
tion and a new beginning." They went to others who had nothing
but the vaguest fatalism for a religion, and they proclaimed exult-
ingly the love of the eternal Father. They went to desolate and
weak and lonely souls, and with shouts of confidence exclaimed,
"Lift up your heads! You can do all things through Christ who
strengthens you." They went to others shivering in cold terror at
the thought of death's onward inexorable march, and they bade
them "Rejoice! Christ has conquered. Death lies dead!" It is the
same tremendous tidings for which the world is hungry yet. To discover, after a hundred defeats, that it is still possible in Christ to
make a fresh beginning; to have distrusted God for half a lifetime
of prayerless years, and then to be told that He cares intensely, and
that the way to His heart lies open now; to have felt utterly inade-
quate for life's demands and for the wear and tear of worrying
days, and then to learn of vast incalculable reserves of power just
waiting to be used; to have had nothing to look forward to but the
snapping of the ties that matter most, and then to find that death
has ceased to count, because victory and immortality belong to
love—this is the glorious news, too often, alas, made dull and
commonplace by our poor bungling, and desupernaturalised by
our stolidity and ineptitude. . . .

. . . There is no reason why your ministry, in its own degree, should not achieve visible results, provided you keep alive within you a sense of the wonder of the facts you preach and of the urgency of the issues with which you deal. Every Sunday morning when it comes ought to find you awed and thrilled by the reflection—"God is to be in action to-day, through me, for these people: this day may be crucial, this service decisive, for someone now ripe for the vision of Jesus." Remember that every soul before you has its own story of need, and that if the Gospel of Christ does not meet such need nothing on earth can. Aim at results. Expect mighty works to happen. Realize that, although your congregation may be small, every soul is infinitely precious. Never forget that Christ Himself, according to His promise, is in the midst, making the plainest and most ordinary church building into the house of God and the gate of heaven. Hear His voice saying, "This day is the Scripture fulfilled in your ears. This day is salvation come to this house." Then preaching, which might otherwise be a dead formality and a barren routine, an implicit denial of its own high claim, will become a power and a passion; and the note of strong, decisive reality, like a trumpet, will awaken the souls of men.

PART TWO
Approaches to Preaching

1

G. Campbell Morgan
1863-1945

G. Campbell Morgan was an active preacher who pastored churches in England and the United States. From 1901-1904 he served as Northfield Bible Conference lecturer in the United States. From 1916-1929 he was an itinerant preacher. In those days many pastors and preachers would testify that their sermon preparation included reading G. Campbell Morgan.

Morgan lectured on preaching in the early 1920s while he was President of Cheshunt College, Cambridge. The lectures were later published under the title **Preaching**. *The four lectures were titled "The Essentials of a Sermon," "The Text," "The Central Message," and "The Introduction and Conclusion." This excerpt from Morgan's first lecture serves as a transition from the "Nature of Preaching" to "Approaches to Preaching."**

The supreme work of the Christian minister is the work of preaching. This is a day in which one of our greatest perils is that of doing a thousand little things to the neglect of the one thing, which is preaching.

I commend the gathering together of all the words in the New Testament—and of course I mean the Greek New Testament—that refer to the exercise of speech for the impartation of truth. We find

* G. Campbell Morgan, *Preaching* (1955; reprint ed., Grand Rapids: Baker Book House, 1974), pp. 11-30, 32-38.

eight or ten different Greek words, every one indicating some phase of this work of preaching. There are two however which are supreme. In our translations they are not always made distinct. All the rest are incidental, though valuable. *Euaggelizo* and *kerusso* are the words which indicate the supreme phases of our preaching, and show us the whole New Testament ideal thereof.

Euaggelizo means to preach the Gospel. The one word is translated by our phrase, "preach the Gospel." Literally it means the proclamation of good news. It is the word from which we derive our words "evangel," "evangelist," and "evangelistic," which come directly by transliteration, rather than by translation, from the Greek word.

If preaching is proclaiming good news, that suggests two things: the need of man, and the grace of God. Those two things are postulated by the very word that is used to describe preaching from the New Testament standpoint. Proclamation of the good news to men will suggest that men are needing good news. Human need is the background. All the race's sin and sorrow and perplexity are implied. Then, of course, it recognizes the whole fact of grace, that stupendous fact of Divine revelation, the grace of God. Preaching as proclaiming good news postulates human need and Divine grace. Whenever we preach, we stand between those two things, between human need and Divine grace. We are the messengers of that grace to that need.

The other word, *kerusso*, is a very interesting term, meaning really a proclamation from a throne. The word is spoken as being delivered by a messenger on behalf of a ruler. Consequently in the use of the word we have two ideas again to note: the authorizing Throne, and therefore the consequent claim that the messenger is called upon to make.

Merge these two things very briefly. What is preaching? It has a hundred particulars and varieties and intonations. But here is the unifying thought. Preaching is the declaration of the grace of God to human need on the authority of the Throne of God; and it demands on the part of those who hear that they show obedience to the thing declared.

I once heard a man at a ministerial conference say: "In the old days preaching was a conflict between the preacher and the crowd. He was in the presence of the crowd to compel the crowd to submission. That day has gone. The preacher's vocation has changed." I wonder! I think, if preaching has failed, or if it is failing, that is why.

The preacher should never address a crowd without remembering that his ultimate citadel is the citadel of the human will. He may travel along the line of the emotions, but he is after the will. He may approach along the line of the intellect, but he is after the will. When preaching becomes merely discussion in the realm of the intellect, or—forgive my use of the word—fooling in the realm of the emotions, and when preaching ends in the intellectual or emotional, it fails. It is successful only when it is able to storm the will, under the will of God. The preacher comes with good news; but he does not come with something to be trifled with. His message has an insistent demand, because he comes from a King.

That is our principal work in the Christian ministry. The apostles said: "We will continue stedfastly in prayer, and in the service (or ministry) of the Word" (Acts 6:4). That was the origin of the order of the New Testament deacons. Whatever the deacons may be now, that tells what they were then. In the New Testament they were men full of faith and the Holy Spirit. Mark the principle of appointing Church officers in the first Churches. Their business was to serve tables, a great ministry, in order that ministers of the Word might be free to serve the Word and to give themselves to prayer in preparation.

I am deeply conscious of the baldness of human speech, but the bigness of the work if we are to be preachers will at once be recognised. Preaching is a great thing. Bishop Frazer said some few years ago—and I think it is more true to-day than it was then: "This age wants, demands, and is prepared to receive, not the priest, but the prophet."

We are facing to-day the biggest hour the world has ever known for preaching. The miseries of theological controversy that are blighting our age cannot satisfy. The mass of men are waiting for preaching of the New Testament kind, with a great message of grace to meet human need, delivered by men who realise that they represent a Throne, and have the right to claim submission to it.

I want to indicate now the essentials of a sermon, and the essentials of sermonizing. These essentials are Truth, Clarity, Passion.

I am speaking out of my experience. I never heard a lecture on homiletics in my life. I have given a good many. One fine preparation for lecturing on homiletics is never to have heard anybody else do it! I have tried to examine in the New Testament, and in the Old Testament, the great preaching of both the prophets of the Old and the apostles and evangelists of the New. And if I am asked to condense into words the essentials of a sermon, I do it with these three: Truth, Clarity, Passion.

I use this word *Truth* now in one way. In writing to Timothy,

Paul charged him in that final letter, so poignant and yet so wonderful, "Preach the Word." The verb means to proclaim as a her-
ald, with authority. His message was to be the Word. Take the
phrase, "the word," and examine its use in the New Testament.
There are some places where it is spelled with a capital W, and
elsewhere it is spelled without a capital W. Why is it spelled with a
capital W here, and without a capital W there?

We read in John, in that matchless Prologue:

"In the beginning was the Word, and the Word was with God,
and the Word was God."

And then, skipping the parenthesis:

"And the Word became flesh."

We find a capital W in every case.

Then we turn to the Gospel of Luke, and read that great Preface,
so important to all the historical documents in our Bible, and he
speaks of those who were "eyewitnesses and ministers of the word."
Here we find a small w. Why the difference? If I am asked, Why
have the translators rendered it with a small w here, instead of a
capital? my answer is, I do not know. There is no reason why. We
have the definite article in both places. "The word" is Luke's last
name for the Son of man. Of course a preface is always written last.
He wrote this preface after the Gospel was written, to introduce it
to his friend Theophilus, and in it he calls Jesus "the Word."

What does this word mean? Bear with me if I condense by
quoting from one of my books:

"The word Logos is used in the New Testament in two ways, the
suggestiveness of each never being wholly absent from the other. Its
first and perhaps simplest meaning is that of speech and language,
the expression of truth for the understanding of others. Its second
and perhaps deeper meaning is that of the absolute truth itself. As
Thayer indicates, in that sense the Greek word *Logos* is the exact
equivalent of the Latin word *Ratio*, from which we obtain our
words *rational* and *reason*. Note the significance of that. Thus
Logos is speech, and the truth spoken, or reason, and the explanation of its expression. The inter-relation of ideas in their use is that
the Word incarnate was the truth of God, but being the speech of
God, was the expression of eternal truth. The Word and reason
must express the idea in a speech which is logical and true. It is
necessary, in the study of the New Testament, carefully to dis-
criminate by reference to the context as to which sense is intended
when this word is used. Sometimes it refers to speech as a statement
made, sometimes to the essential truth out of which the statement

came, sometimes both ideas are most evidently present in the use of the word."

It will be granted that preachers are to preach the Word. You say that means the Bible. Does it? Yes. Is that all? No. Yes, it is all there. But you want more than that, more than all. The Word is truth as expressed or revealed. The Word is never something that I have found out by the activity of my own intellectual life. The Word is something which my intellectual life apprehends, because it has been expressed. If we take the 119th Psalm and study it through—that great psalm concerning the Word of God—we are not to imagine that it is referring only to the *Torah* or Law, the *Nebiim* or Prophets, the *Kethubim* or Writings. It has in view the truth, the essential truth, and the truth as God makes it known. All that is focused in Christ for us as preachers; and Christ is revealed to us through this literature.

But it may be asked: Isn't there an experience of Christ? There is, but the literature tests the experience. That was a tremendous description that Justin Martyr gave when, speaking of the Word of God, he referred to "the spermatic Word." Seed, that is to say, the truth in germ and norm. That is what we have in the Christ, and which we find in our Bible—germ and norm.

Apply that to the Bible; what then have we? Truth in germ, which needs apprehension, development, application. That is the work of the preacher. But we also have it in norm. This means that we are to test our own thinking by it finally, and not it by our own thinking. Consequently the preacher is to be held by the Word, truth, as it is in God, and as God has made it known. How has He made it known? We are assuming without any argument that God has made it known finally in His Son, and that in literature, the Biblical literature, we have the full record of preparation, of historic fact, of initial interpretation. Follow the line of that. Preparation, all the Old Testament. Historic fact, the four Gospel narratives. Initial interpretation, all the twenty-one letters. There we have all the literature around this one great Person, Who is in that sense for us the Word.

And that is what we have to preach. God's revelation, the truth, as it has been expressed. We must enter upon the Christian ministry on the assumption that God has expressed Himself in His Son, and that the Bible is the literature of that self-expression. The minute we lose our Bible in that regard, we have lost Christ as the final revelation. I don't want to be controversial, but you will find it is always so. Let me speak with profound respect of the men who have suffered this loss. Here is a man who for some reason refuses the authority of his Bible, but says he will stand by Christ. What Christ?

There is a fashion to-day among some preachers, to talk and preach about the approach to Jesus. We are being told that we must go back and approach Him as His early disciples did. Did we ever realise the utter fallacy of that position? Those men apprehended Him in the days of His limitation, when He Himself had to say:

> I came to cast fire upon the earth; and what do I desire, if it is already kindled? But I have a baptism to be baptized with; and how am I straitened till it be accomplished! (Luke 12:49, 50).

Ponder the significance of that—Christ's great soliloquy in this chapter in Luke in which He expressed His difficulty, that He could not make Himself known, could not fulfill His mission. He was straitened. The teaching of Christ is not the final fact about Christ, and His Person is not the final fact about Christ. We find that fact in Jesus crucified, risen, and ascended. We must approach Christ thus and we must cling to that Christ. That is the Word of God in all its fullness.

Every sermon, then, is a message out of that sum totality of truth. Any sermon that fails to have some interpretation of that holy truth is a failure. That totality is not a small thing. In Him are summed up all things. In Him dwells the fullness, the *pleroma*, of the Godhead corporeally. The man who begins to preach Christ as the Divine revelation interpreted to him through the literature, is beginning a thing that will never end. He can never be at the end of his message, because his message is the infinite and full and eternal truth. Preaching is the declaration of truth, as truth has been revealed to men by God, in Christ.

Take the word "mystery" as we find it in the New Testament. What do we mean by a mystery? Ordinarily it means something that we cannot understand. The Greek philosopher meant by it something that can be made known only to the initiated, and which, being made known, cannot be told to any other than those initiated. That is not the meaning of "mystery" in the New Testament. There, a mystery is something which human intellect can apprehend when it is revealed. "Great is the mystery of godliness." Paul does not mean godliness is something we cannot understand. The deep heart and meaning of godliness is beyond the discovery of the human intellect; it is something revealed. Put "manifest" over against "mystery." Being manifested, it can be apprehended.

Here is our richness, if we are going to preach. The preacher is a steward of the mysteries of God, not things that cannot be apprehended, but things that human intellect cannot discover, which God has revealed. The New Testament preacher is always moving in the realm of the supernatural. It is absurd for a man to say that he rules out the supernatural when he cuts out the little things he calls miracles—I mean little by comparison. All the miracles of Jesus, what men call miracles, are very secondary and unimportant compared with what He said, and finally insignificant by the side of Himself and His mighty Word. The words of Jesus are far more supernatural than the things He did, if by miracle we mean some activity in the realms of the material things. We have to deal with the supernatural. All preachers must. Preachers have been told that they have been too other-worldly. When we cease to be other-worldly we lose our ability to touch this world with any healing and uplifting power. We move in the realm of truth revealed, coming to men from God.

That forces us to distinguish. Preaching is not the proclamation of a theory, or the discussion of a doubt. A man has a perfect right to proclaim a theory of any sort, or to discuss his doubts. But that is not preaching. "Give me the benefit of your convictions, if you have any. Keep your doubts to yourself; I have enough of my own," said Goethe. We are never preaching when we are hazarding speculations. Of course we do so. We are bound to speculate sometimes. I sometimes say: "I am speculating; stop taking notes." Speculation is not preaching. Neither is the declaration of negations preaching. Preaching is the proclamation of the Word, the truth as the truth has been revealed.

Our deposit is the sum totality of the truth. We are holding a bigger thing than we know. If we should live and preach for half a century or a century, we should never be able to exhaust the thing that is ours as a deposit. Paul wrote:

> I know Whom I have believed, and I am persuaded that He is able to guard that which I have committed unto Him against that day.

I am not so sure that this is correct translation. It is an attempt to interpret. It is literally translated, "to guard my deposit." Our translators have always made it mean something Paul had deposited with Him. I think it means rather that which He had deposited with Paul, the thing for which he was responsible; this whole truth, this Word of God, focussed, crystallised in a Person, and interpreted by a literature.

That is our business as preachers. "Oh, but the preacher must catch the spirit of the age." God forgive him if he does. Our business is never to catch, but by eternal truth to correct the spirit of the age. This is not narrow. Nothing can happen to-day to which the truth of God has not something to say. Our preaching will touch life at every point. We do not go to discuss a situation, but to deliver a message. The preacher must for evermore stand in the presence of man and conditions, thinking in his own soul, if the formula is not often upon his lips, "Thus saith the Lord." Here is the truth, the truth that men never have been able to discover by all the exercise, honest and sincere and persistent, of their intellectual activity, but the truth that God has spoken, revealed, made known. (See Hebrews 1:1-4.) He has spoken to us in a Son. The great fact is God, God speaking, making Himself known in the past in divers portions and by divers manners, at last in a Person, Who gathered up the portions and uttered them in one inclusive final revelation. When we enter the Christian ministry and become preachers, it is that whole body of truth for which we are responsible.

By truth I mean the Word, in all the fullness of the suggestiveness of that expression. May I say again that by that I mean the revelation, God's Self-revelation of Himself, centrally, supremely, finally in His Son. But, of course, also in the literature that is in the Bible. Preaching is declaring the truth of God as it bears upon every local situation. "Preach the Word."

As I said, every sermon is an interpretation, or should be an interpretation, of some part of that great whole of truth. Every sermon is characterized by two things—originality and authority.

I am going to make a long quotation. Some thirty-five or more years ago I wrote this out for myself, and I have kept it by me, and very often have read it. It is on *originality*. Men were constantly using that term "original," insisting that the preacher must be original. We have heard it said in criticism of a sermon, "It was very good, but it was not original." We should realise what originality really is, therefore I give this somewhat lengthy quotation from Shedd:

> Originality is a term often employed, rarely defined, and very often misunderstood. It is frequently supposed to be equivalent to the creation of truth. An original mind, it is vulgarly imagined, is one that gives expression to ideas and truths that were never heard of before,—ideas and truths of which the human mind never had even an intimation or presentiment, and which come into it by a mortal leap, abrupt and startling, without antecedents and without pre-

monitions. But no such originality as this is possible to a finite intelligence. Such aboriginality as this is the prerogative of the Creator alone, and the results of it are a *revelation*, in the technical and strict sense of the term. Only God can create *de nihilo*, and only God can make a communication of truth that is absolutely new. Originality in man is always relative, and never absolute. Select, for illustration, an original thinker within the province of philosophy,—select the contemplative, the profound, the ever fresh and living Plato. Thoughtfully peruse his weighty and his musical periods, and ask yourself whether all this wisdom is the sheer make of his intellectual energy, or whether it is not rather an emanation and efflux from a mental *constitution* which is as much yours as his. He did not absolutely originate these first truths of ethics, these necessary forms of logic, these fixed principles of physics. They were inlaid in his rational structure by a higher author, and by an absolute authorship; and his originality consists solely in their exegesis and interpretation. And this is the reason that, on listening to his words, we do not seem to be hearing tones that are wholly unknown and wholly unheard of. We find an answering voice to them in our mental and moral constitution. In no contemptuous, but in a reverential and firm tone, every thinking person, even in the presence of the great thinkers of the race, may employ the language of Job, in reference to self-evident truths and propositions:

> Lo, mine eye hath seen all this, mine ear hath
>   heard and understood it.
> What ye know, the same do I know also; I am
>   not inferior unto you.

This quotation from Job is wonderfully apt at this point. Every one who listens to us when we are giving him something original is saying that thing.

And these great thinkers themselves are the first to acknowledge this. . . . Originality, then, within the sphere of a creature, and in reference to a finite intelligence, consists in the power of interpretation. In its last analysis it is *exegesis*,—the pure, genial, and accurate exposition of an idea or a truth already existing, already communicated, already possessed. . . . There has been no creation, but only a development; no absolute authorship, but only an explication. And yet how fresh and original has been the mental process! The same substantially in Plato and in the thousands of his scholars; and yet in every single instance there has been all the enthusiasm, all the stimulation, all the ebullient flow of life and feeling that attends the discovery of a new continent or a new star.

> Then feels he like some watcher of the skies
>   When a new plant swims into his ken;
> Or like stout Cortez, when with eagle eyes
>   He stared at the Pacific, and all his men
> Looked at each other with a wild surmise,
>   Silent, upon a peak in Darien.

Originality in man, then, is not the power of making a communication of truth, but of apprehending one. Two great communications have been made to him,—the one in the book of nature, and the other in the book of revelation. If the truth has been conveyed through the mental and moral structure, if it has been wrought by the creative hand into the fabric of human nature, then he is the most original thinker who is most successful in reading it just as it reads, and expounding it just as it stands. If the truth has been communicated by miracle, by incarnation, and by the Holy Ghost; if it has been imparted by special inspiration, and lies before him an objective and written revelation; then he is the original thinker who is most successful in its interpretation,—who is most accurate in analysing its living elements, and is most genial and cordial in receiving them into his own mental and moral being.

This quotation is one of the statements that have profoundly influenced my life, my working, and my preaching. We see where that takes the question of originality. If indeed, our deposit as preachers is that sum total of truth, contained in the Word, which we face in order to interpret, in the written Word, we shall always be original. Not that we are inventing new truths, or even discovering them, but that we are interpreting the sum total of truth by every Christian sermon that has in it the originality of the apprehension of the meaning of revealed truth, and of giving it to others that they might apprehend it. That originality is a note of real preaching. A man who is merely indulging in speculation, along the ways of his own thinking, is never original. Originality in preaching consists in the interpretation of revelation. Revelation is so great and mighty, that if we are dealing with that, and always leading into it, in every message, there is always something original in our preaching.

A sermon should be characterized also by *authority*. In the seventh chapter of Matthew there is a little paragraph which Matthew wrote with reference to the effect produced upon the multitude by what we call the Sermon on the Mount—rather the great ethical manifesto of the King—concerning the effect upon the multitude:

And it came to pass, when Jesus had finished these words, the multitudes were astonished at His teaching; for He taught them as One having authority, and not as their scribes (Matt. 7:28, 29).

Has it ever occurred to us that the remarkable thing is not the declaration that He spake as One having authority, though that is the main thing? What arrests us?

> The multitudes were astonished at His teaching; for He taught them
> as One having authority, and *not as their scribes.*

The arresting thing in that statement is the little phrase which
makes that distinction or contrast. I could read it over and over
again, and agree. Of course, when He spake He had authority. But
the thing that arrested me long ago and still holds me is the contrast suggested, "not as their scribes."

The scribes were the authoritative teachers. An order of scribes
was not arranged for in the Mosaic economy. They came with
Ezra. When Ezra erected that pulpit of wood, and held what we
can probably call the first Bible conference of record, he "read the
law, and gave the sense." This means first that he was translating it
from Hebrew into the language of the captivity; but it means more.
He interpreted and applied it. So arose the order of scribes. Their
work was that of moral interpretation. They were the authoritative
teachers, whom our Lord recognized. In Matthew 23 He said:

> The scribes and the Pharisees sit on Moses' seat; all things therefore
> whatsoever they bid you, these do and observe—

but don't do as they do. That is a startling thing. While not appointed in the Mosaic economy at the beginning, their authority
was recognized, and our Lord also acknowledged it. They surely
spoke with authority. And yet Matthew says; "He spoke as One
having authority but not as the scribes."

The authority detected in the teaching of Jesus was not of the
nature of the authority detected in the teachings of the scribes.
What was the difference? The authority of the scribes consisted in
their recognized position, in the fact that they were chosen to be the
interpreters of the Law of Moses. It was the authority of the office
conferred and exercised. What was the difference? He spoke as One
having authority, but not that way. I do not think this authority
was to be found in His demeanor, in His attitude, in His look,
though I don't think, if we had seen our Lord in the days of His
flesh and listened to Him, we would have missed the dignity and
wonder of His personality. His authority was rather the authority
of the thing He said, as it found them and found in them an answer
of acquiescence. . . .

Again every sermon should have *clarity.* Of course I mean clarity of statement in every way. Martin Luther said: "A preacher
ought so to preach, that when the sermon is ended, the congregation shall disperse saying, 'The preacher said this.' "

The whole point, as I understand it, is that the sermon should have a message that is perfectly clear in its statement of something that grips the congregation, so that they would go away saying, "The preacher said this." Clarity. In preaching everything should be subservient to this.

Here another thing to be remembered is, that the making plain does not depend upon us finally, but upon the Holy Spirit. The preaching of the Word must be in the demonstration and power of the Holy Spirit, not power only, but demonstration, the making plain. When the Christian preacher, preaching out of His Word, is true to His will, he may know that in cooperation with him—I use the word reverently, but reasonably—is the Holy Spirit making the Word plain. But no man has any right to depend wholly upon that. In the preparation and delivery of a sermon we must be very careful that we make our statement such as can be apprehended by those who are listening. That applies to diction, illustrations, and manner of delivery. We preach in order that people may apprehend. . . .

Clarity affects the whole question of illustrations. That is another big side issue, but I would give to every young preacher a simple formula for his illustrations. Let your illustrations be such as shine into your sermon, and not illustrations that you drag in. You have heard men preach, and tell a story. The story has really no vital relationship with their message. They put it in, and it relieves the congregation, making them smile at the moment, perhaps, but it has no relation to the sermon. One of the most skillful in this matter that I have known was John Henry Jowett. W. L. Watkinson was another. Dr. Jowett's illustrations always shone into his main theme. You never went away with the illustration as the supreme thing; it was there illuminating. I remember hearing him in Birmingham, when he said: "Human and Divine divisions of humanity are radically different. Divine divisions are perpendicular, human divisions are horizontal."

Well, there we were. He picked up his hymn book, held it upright, and said: "I will show you what I mean. That is perpendicular division to the right, to the left; that is Divine."

Then holding it flat; "This is horizontal—upper, middle, lower classes; that is human."

That is great illustration.

With the portion of truth that is constituting the sermon, with the great originality that is always in an inescapable truth, winged with its own authority, our business is in some way to make that truth have clarity in our diction, in our illustration, and of course in our manner.

Finally there is a third essential, *Passion*. I want to say a word about this quite briefly. In the true sermon there must always be passion. But the passion must be something that is created by no conscious effort. It must come out of what we are declaring, and out of our consciousness of it. Half the sermons to-day—may I be forgiven if I am cruel—are failing because they lack the note of passion. . . .

I am not arguing for mere excitement. Painted fire never burns, and an imitated enthusiasm is the most empty thing that can possibly exist in a preacher. Given the preacher with a message from the whole Bible, seeing its bearing on life at any point, I cannot personally understand that man not being swept sometimes right out of himself by the fire and the force and the fervour of his work.

Truth, clarity, passion—I believe that in the real sermon these three things are always found.

Truth will always, in my view, make its impression of authority upon the soul, but we cannot get it over to the soul save as it comes through our own personality, not merely as an intellectual concept, but as a thing that is moving us. I don't think any preacher ever can lift his hearers above the level of his own experience. That is a great conviction with me. We cannot take our people, even if we state truth accurately, if it is only an intellectual statement, and make them feel its force. That is the difference between the press and the pulpit. Read a book, and we have the truth, perhaps, but in preaching you have the truth plus the man, not plus as though we can separate them, but the truth incarnate expressing itself to me through man.

Truth and life travel together in preaching. He Who said, "I am the truth," also said, "I am the life." In Him we have the eternal illustration of the power of truth in life. In a measure that has to be reproduced in all who are really preaching. Of course, it is a very different thing from lecturing, or discussing things with the congregation. That does not concern us. Our business is uttering the Word of God.

2
Charles H. Spurgeon
1834-1892

Few men in history have preached weekly to as many people as Charles H. Spurgeon. In 1854 Spurgeon was called to his second pastorate, the New Park Street Church in London. Seven years later the six-thousand seat Metropolitan Tabernacle opened, but even this church was not large enough to accommodate all who wanted to hear him.

*Why was Spurgeon such a popular preacher? The most prominent reasons are: he was a biblical preacher; he was a master of the use of sensory appeal in his preaching; and he spoke strongly, clearly, and naturally. Spurgeon's approach to preaching is clearly given in his **Lectures to My Students**. There are twenty-seven lectures in the book. The topics range from personal, spiritual matters to "Astronomy as a Source of Illustration." The following excerpt is from the lecture titled "Sermons: Their Matter."* Spurgeon spoke incisively and with delightful wit; therefore, it was unnecessary and unwise to attempt to edit the material.*

——— —— ———

Sermons should have real teaching in them, and their doctrine should be solid, substantial, and abundant. We do not enter the pulpit to talk for talk's sake; we have instructions to convey, important to the last degree, and we cannot afford to utter pretty nothings. Our range of subjects is all but boundless, and we cannot,

---

* Charles H. Spurgeon, *Lectures to My Students* (1875; reprint ed., Grand Rapids: Baker Book House, 1977), pp. 72-83.

therefore, be excused if our discourses are threadbare and devoid of substance. If we speak as ambassadors for God, we need never complain of want of matter, for our message is full to overflowing. The entire gospel must be presented from the pulpit; the whole faith once delivered to the saints must be proclaimed by us. The truth as it is in Jesus must be instructively declared, so that the people may not merely hear, but know, the joyful sound. We serve not at the altar of "the unknown God," but we speak to the worshipers of Him of whom it is written, "they that know thy name will put their trust in thee."

To divide a sermon well may be a very useful art, but how if there is nothing to divide? A mere division maker is like an excellent carver with an empty dish before him. To be able to deliver an exordium which shall be appropriate and attractive, to be at ease in speaking with propriety during the time allotted for the discourse, and to wind up with a respectable peroration, may appear to mere religious performers to be all that is requisite; but the true minister of Christ knows that the true value of a sermon must lie, not in its fashion and manner, but in the truth which it contains.

Nothing can compensate for the absence of teaching; all the rhetoric in the world is but as chaff to the wheat in contrast to the Gospel of our salvation. However beautiful the sower's basket, it is a miserable mockery if it be without seed. The grandest discourse ever delivered is an ostentatious failure if the doctrine of the grace of God be absent from it; it sweeps over men's heads like a cloud, but it distributes no rain upon the thirsty earth; and therefore the remembrance of it to souls taught wisdom by an experience of pressing need is one of disappointment or worse. A man's style may be as fascinating as that of the authoress of whom one said, "that she should write with a crystal pen dipped in dew upon silver paper, and use for pounce the dust of a butterfly's wing"; but to an audience whose souls are in instant jeopardy, what will mere elegance be but "altogether lighter than vanity"?

Horses are not to be judged by their bells or their trappings, but by limb and bone and blood; and sermons, when criticized by judicious hearers, are largely measured by the amount of Gospel truth and force of Gospel spirit which they contain. Brethren, weigh your sermons. Do not retail them by the yard, but deal them out by the pound. Set no store by the quantity of words which you utter, but strive to be esteemed for the quality of your matter. It is foolish to be lavish in words and niggardly in truth. He must be very destitute of wit who would be pleased to hear himself described after the manner of the world's great poet, who says, "Gratiano speaks an infinite deal of nothing, more than any man in all Venice. His reason are as two grains of wheat hid in two bushels of chaff: you shall seek all day ere you find them, and when you have them, they are not worth the search." . . .

Sound information upon Scriptural subjects your hearers crave for, and must have. Accurate explanations of Holy Scripture they are entitled to, and if you are "an interpreter, one among a thousand," a real messenger of heaven, you will yield them plenteously. Whatever else may be present, the absence of edifying, instructive truth, like the absence of flour from bread, will be fatal. Estimated by their solid contents rather than their superficial area, many sermons are very poor specimens of godly discourse.

I believe the remark is too well-grounded that if you attend to a lecturer on astronomy or geology, during a short course you will obtain a tolerably clear view of his system; but if you listen, not only for twelve months, but for twelve years, to the common run of preachers, you will not arrive at anything like an idea of their system of theology. If it be so, it is a grievous fault, which cannot be too much deplored. Alas, the indistinct utterances of many concerning the grandest of eternal realities, and the dimness of thought in others with regard to fundamental truths, have given too much occasion for the criticism!

Brethren, if you are not theologians you are in your pastorates just nothing at all. You may be fine rhetoricians, and be rich in polished sentences; but without knowledge of the Gospel, and aptness to teach it, you are but a "sounding brass, or a tinkling cymbal." Verbiage is too often the fig leaf which does duty as a covering for theological ignorance. Sounding periods are offered instead of sound doctrine, and rhetorical flourishes in the place of robust thought. Such things ought not to be. The abounding of empty declamation, and the absence of food for the soul, will turn a pulpit into a box of bombast, and inspire contempt instead of reverence. Unless we are instructive preachers, and really feed the people, we may be great quoters of elegant poetry, and mighty retailers of second-hand wind-bags, but we shall be like Nero of old, fiddling while Rome was burning, and sending vessels to Alexandria to fetch sand for the arena while the populace starved for want of corn.

We insist upon it, that there must be abundance of matter in sermons, and next, that this matter must be congruous to the text. The discourse should spring out of the text as a rule, and the more evidently it does so the better; but at all times, to say the least, it should have very close relationship thereto . . . .

Some brethren have done with their text as soon as they have read it. Having paid all due honor to that particular passage by announcing it, they feel no necessity further to refer to it. They touch their hats, as it were, to that part of Scripture, and pass on to fresh fields and pastures new. Why do such men take a text at all? Why limit their own glorious liberty? Why make Scripture a horsing-block by which to mount upon their unbridled Pegasus? Surely the words of inspiration were never meant to be boothooks to help a Talkative to draw on his seven-leagued boots in which to leap from pole to pole . . . .

Take care that your deliverances are always weighty, and full of really important teaching. Build not with wood, hay and stubble, but with gold, silver and precious stones. It is scarcely needful to warn you against the grosser degradation of pulpit eloquence, or the example of the notorious orator Henley might be instanced. That loquacious adventurer, whom Pope has immortalized in his *Dunciad*, was wont to make the passing events of the week the themes of his buffoonery on week days, and theological topics suffered the same fate on Sundays. His forte lay in his low wit and in tuning his voice and balancing his hands. The satirist says of him, "How fluent nonsense trickles from his tongue." Gentlemen, it were better never to have been born, than to have the like truthfully said of us; we are in peril of our souls bound to deal with the solemnities of eternity and with no earth-born topics . . . .

It is infamous to ascend your pulpit and pour over your people rivers of language, cataracts of words, in which mere platitudes are held in solution like infinitesimal grains of homeopathic medicine in an Atlantic of utterance. Better far give the people masses of unprepared truth in the rough, like pieces of meat from a butcher's block, chopped off anyhow, bone and all, and even dropped down in the sawdust, than ostentatiously and delicately hand them out upon a china dish a delicious slice of nothing at all, decorated with the parsley of poetry, and flavored with the sauce of affectation.

It will be a happy circumstance if you are so guided by the Holy Spirit as to give a clear testimony to all the doctrines which constitute or lie around the Gospel. No truth is to be kept back. The doctrine of reserve, so detestable in the mouths of Jesuits, is not one whit the less villainous when accepted by Protestants. It is not true that some doctrines are only for the initiated; there is nothing in the Bible which is ashamed of the light. The sublimest vows of divine sovereignty have a practical bearing, and are not, as some think, mere metaphysical subtleties; the distinctive utterances of Calvinism have their bearing upon everyday life and ordinary experience, and if you hold such views, or the opposite, you have no dispensation permitting you to conceal your beliefs. Cautious reticence is, in nine cases out of ten, cowardly betrayal. The best policy is never to be politic, but to proclaim every atom of the truth so far as God has taught it to you.

Harmony requires that the voice of one doctrine shall not drown the rest, and it also demands that the gentler notes shall not be omitted because of the greater volume of other sounds. Every note appointed by the great minstrel must be sounded; each note having its own proportionate power and emphasis, the passage marked with *forte* must not be softened, and those with *piano* must not be rolled out like thunder, but each must have its due hearing. All revealed truth in harmonious proportion must be your theme . . . .

We must throw all our strength of judgment, memory, imagination, and eloquence into the delivery of the Gospel; and not give to the preaching of the Cross our random thoughts while wayside topics engross our deeper meditations. Depend upon it, if we brought the intellect of a Locke or a Newton, and the eloquence of a Cicero, to bear upon the simple doctrine of "believe and live," we should find no surplus strength. Brethren, first and above all things, keep to plain evangelical doctrines; whatever else you do or do not preach, be sure incessantly to bring forth the soul-saving truth of Christ and Him crucified.

I know a minister whose shoe latchet I am unworthy to unloose, whose preaching is often little better than sacred miniature painting—I might almost say holy trifling. He is great upon the ten toes of the beast, the four faces of the cherubim, the mystical meaning of badgers' skins, and the typical bearings of the staves of the ark, and the windows of Solomon's temple: but the sins of business men, the temptations of the times, and the needs of the age, he scarcely ever touches upon. Such preaching reminds me of a lion engaged in mouse-hunting, or a man-of-war cruising after a lost water-butt.

Topics scarcely in importance equal to what Peter calls "old wives' fables," are made great matters by those microscopic divines to whom the nicety of a point is more attractive than the saving of souls. You will have read in Todd's *Student's Manual* that Harcatius, king of Persia, was a notable mole-catcher; and Briantes, king of Lydia, was equally *au fait* at filing needles; but these trivialities by no means prove them to have been great kings:

it is much the same in the ministry; there is such a thing as mean-
ness of mental occupation unbecoming the rank of an ambassador
of heaven.

Among a certain order of minds at this time the Athenian desire
of telling or hearing some new things appears to be predominant.
They boast of new light, and claim a species of inspiration which
warrants them in condemning all who are out of their brotherhood, and yet their grand revelation relates to a mere circum-
stantiality of worship or to an obscure interpretation of prophecy;
so that, at sight of their great fuss and loud cry concerning so little,
we are reminded of—

> Ocean into tempest toss'd
> To waft a feather or to drown a fly.

Worse still are those who waste time in insinuating doubts concerning the authenticity of texts, or the correctness of Biblical
statements concerning natural phenomena. Painfully do I call to
mind hearing one Sabbath evening a deliverance called a sermon,
of which the theme was a clever inquiry as to whether an angel did
actually descend and stir the pool at Bethesda, or whether it was an
intermitting spring, concerning which Jewish superstition had invented a legend. Dying men and women were assembled to hear
the way of salvation, and they were put off with such vanity as this!
They came for bread, and received a stone; the sheep looked up to
the shepherd, and were not fed. Seldom do I hear a sermon, and
when I do I am grievously unfortunate, for one of the last I was en-
tertained with was intended to be a justification of Joshua for destroying the Canaanites, and another went to prove that it was not
good for man to be alone. How many souls were converted in answer to the prayers before these sermons I have never been able to
ascertain, but I shrewdly suspect that no unusual rejoicing dis-
turbed the serenity of the golden streets.

Believing my next remark to be almost universally unneeded, I
bring it forward with diffidence—do not overload a sermon with
too much matter. All truth is not to be comprised in one discourse.

Sermons are not to be bodies of divinity. There is such a thing as
having too much to say, and saying it till hearers are sent home
loathing rather than longing. An old minister walking with a
young preacher, pointed to a cornfield, and observed, "Your last
sermon had too much in it, and it was not clear enough, or sufficiently well-arranged; it was like that field of corn, it contained

much crude food, but none fit for use. You should make your sermons like a loaf of bread, fit for eating, and in convenient form."

It is to be feared that human heads (speaking phrenologically) are not so capacious for theology as they once were, for our forefathers rejoiced in sixteen ounces of divinity, undiluted and unadorned, and could continue receiving it for three or four hours at a stretch, but our more degenerate, or perhaps more busy, generation requires about an ounce of doctrine at a time, and that must be the concentrated extract or essential oil, rather than the entire substance of divinity. We must in these times say a great deal in a few words, but not too much, nor with too much amplification. One thought fixed on the mind will be better than fifty thoughts made to flit across the ear. One tenpenny nail driven home and clenched will be more useful than a score of tin tacks loosely fixed, to be pulled out again in an hour . . . .

Do not let your thoughts rush as a mob, but make them march as a troop of soldiery. Order, which is heaven's first law, must not be neglected by heaven's ambassadors.

Your doctrinal teaching should be clear and unmistakable. To be so it must first of all be clear to yourself. Some men think in smoke and preach in a cloud. Your people do not want a luminous haze, but the solid *terra firma* of truth. Philosophical speculations put certain minds into a semi-intoxicated condition, in which they either see every thing double, or see nothing at all . . . .

For my part, I believe that the chief readers of heterodox books are ministers, and that if they would not notice them they would fall stillborn from the press. Let a minister keep clear of mystifying himself, and then he is on the road to becoming intelligible to his people. No man can hope to be felt who cannot make himself understood. If we give our people refined truth, pure Scriptural doctrine, and all so worded as to have no needless obscurity about it, we shall be true shepherds of the sheep, and the profiting of our people will soon be apparent . . . .

Let your teachings grow and advance; let them deepen with your experience, and rise with your soul-progress. I do not mean preach new truths; for, on the contrary, I hold that man happy who is so well-taught from the first that, after fifty years of ministry, he has never had to recant a doctrine or to mourn an important omission; but I mean, let our depth and insight continually increase, and where there is spiritual advance it will be so. Timothy could not preach like Paul. Our earlier productions must be surpassed by those of our riper years; we must never make these our models; they will be best burned, or only preserved to be mourned over because of their superficial character.

It were ill, indeed, if we knew no more after being many years in Christ's school; our progress may be slow, but progress there must be, or there will be cause to suspect that the inner life is lacking or sadly unhealthy. Set it before you as most certain that you have not yet attained, and may grace be given you to press forward toward that which is yet beyond. May you all become able ministers of the New Testament, and not a whit behind the very chief of preachers, though in yourselves you will still be nothing.

Of all I would wish to say this is the sum: my brethren, preach *Christ*, always and evermore. He is the whole Gospel. His Person, offices, and work must be our one great, all comprehending theme. The world needs still to be told of its Saviour, and of the way to reach Him. Justification by faith should be far more than it is the daily testimony of Protestant pulpits; and if with this master-truth there should be more generally associated the other great doctrines of grace, the better for our churches and our age.

If with the zeal of Methodists we can preach the doctrine of Puritans, a great future is before us. The fire of Wesley, and the fuel of Whitefield, will cause a burning which shall set the forests of error on fire, and warm the very soul of this cold earth. We are not called to proclaim philosophy and metaphysics, but the simple Gospel. Man's fall, his need of a new birth, forgiveness through an atonement, and salvation as a result of faith—these are our battle-axe and weapons of war. We have enough to do to learn and teach these great truths, and accursed be that learning which shall divert us from our mission . . . .

More and more I am jealous lest any views upon prophecy, church government, politics, or even systematic theology, should withdraw one of us from glorifying in the Cross of Christ. Salvation is a theme for which I would fain enlist every holy tongue. I am greedy after witnesses for the glorious Gospel of the blessed God. O that Christ crucified were the universal burden of men of God. Your guess at the number of the beast, your Napoleonic speculations, your conjectures concerning a personal antichrist—forgive me, I count them but mere bones for dogs; while men are dying, and hell is filling, it seems to me the veriest drivel to be muttering about an Armageddon at Sebastopol or Sadowa or Sedan, and peeping between the folded leaves of destiny to discover the fate of Germany.

Blessed are they who read and hear the words of the prophecy of the Revelation, but the like blessing has evidently not fallen on those who pretend to expound it, for generation after generation of them have been proved to be in error by the mere lapse of time, and the present race will follow to the same inglorious sepulcher. I would sooner pluck one single brand from the burning than explain all mysteries. To win a soul from going down into the pit is a more glorious achievement than to be crowned in the arena of theological controversy as Doctor Sufficientissimus; to have faithfully unveiled the glory of God in the face of Jesus Christ will be in the final judgment accounted worthier service than to have solved the problems of the religious Sphinx, or to have cut the Gordian knot of apocalyptic difficulty. Blessed is that ministry of which *Christ is all.*

3

Joseph Fort Newton
1878-1950

*Joseph Fort Newton wanted to see the church play a more meaningful role in society. This desire moved him from his Southern Baptist roots. He became a Universalist and concluded his ministry as an Episcopalian. City Temple Church in London called him as pastor in 1916 primarily because of his views on the church as expressed in sermons published by **Christian Century**.*

*Newton maintained that preaching should be inductive rather than deductive. That view is reflected in his book, **The New Preaching**.* The first half of the book covers various facets of preaching. The second half is a reevaluation of preaching, something which Newton felt was desperately needed. This excerpt, "The New Strategy," is an excerpt from the second half and deals specifically with the inductive approach.*

——— ● ———

As a matter of strategy, if for no other reason, the new preaching must be inductive in its emphasis and approach. Inevitably so, because the whole spirit and method of thought in our day is inductive, and if we are to win the men of to-day to the truths of faith we must use the method by which they find truth in other fields. In the old days the text was a truth assumed to be true, and the preacher only needed to expound its meaning, deduce its lessons and apply

* Joseph F. Newton, *The New Preaching* (Nashville: Cokesbury Press, 1930), pp. 139-44.

them. Often enough a text was a tiny peg from which a vast weight of theology depended, and so long as men accepted both the text and the theology all went well. Of course, the old formula, "The Bible teaches, therefore it is valid," is still sufficient for those who accept such authorities. But in an age of inquiry, when the authority of the Bible and the Church is questioned by so many, such an appeal does not carry conviction. We may wish it otherwise, but we must face the facts and be wise enough to win men on their own terms, remembering that we are persuaders, not soldiers, fishers of men and not mere critics. Also, if by appeal to the facts of life we can show the truths of faith to be real, we have reestablished the authority of the Bible and the Church.

The inductive method is indispensable in teaching the genetic truths of faith, doubly so in an age when a spongy texture of mind deplores all dogma and loves disembodied ideas that float in vapory phrases in the air, binding us to nothing positive. None the less, as Plato said long ago, because "an unexamined life is unlivable," we must have a theology—building and built upon—else our faith will evaporate in a misty sentiment, or sink into a series of vagrant insights, or become a mere "boneless wonder." But it asks for a fine strategy to make such a deep truth as the Trinity real to the mind of our day, even if it be vital to our faith alike by its meaning and its mystery. If stated as sheer dogma, it wears the aspect of an arid formula, a queer mixture of mysticism, metaphysics, and mathematics, as empty as it is unreal. But if treated inductively, it is unveiled as one of the basic thought-forms of the mind of man in its attempt to interpret the life of God. In Egypt, in India, in many lands and ages, long before our era, humanity thought of God as Father, Mother, Child, as if the life of man were a cup to be filled by the love of God. No wonder the faith which came not to destroy but to fulfill found focus in a vision of God through the family as a society in Himself, making the home an altar of faith and prophecy. And that vision is needed to-day, as never before, to make vivid the truth of the love of God, as well as a basis, both in the need of man and the nature of God, for a real social gospel.

For some time I have been discussing the matter of inductive preaching with my English friends in letters, much to my delight and profit. One of them sent me an example of an inductive sermon so admirable that I venture to pass it along. The preacher wished to make a plea for single-heartedness in the service of God, taking for his text the words of Jesus, "Ye cannot serve God and mammon." Had he used the old method, he would have stated the truth of the text as a proposition and gone straight to his deductions, but he would not have carried his hearers with him. Many men to-day, as all will agree, are unconvinced that such a double service is impossible. Indeed, not a few hold that the great thing in life is precisely a skillful adjustment of the service of God and the service of the world—like the old woman who always curtseyed at the name of the devil "so as to be safe anyhow," and her family is very large. The preacher may have the tongue of an angel, but he will not win men in that way who question the truth of his text at the outset.

By the inductive approach it is different; it puts no weight on the text at first, but begins with near-by facts familiar to all, using popular illustrations. Is it not true that in factory life fatigue and weariness are common? Why? The mind is divided. On the contrary, the theater and the golf game bring the minimum of weariness, in spite of long hours. In the same way, hours spent in pursuing a hobby—growing roses, say—even produces freshness of mind. Why? There is single-hearted enjoyment in the work. "Why, this is true!" is the unspoken verdict; the truth of the text is approved, not only as upon divine authority, but as a truth of experience. Having led his hearers on a tour of exploration, the preacher may now skillfully use a sense of intellectual satisfaction as an opportunity to create a deep sense of spiritual dissatisfaction. Such a method seems to be the best in an age which has a peculiar bent toward discovery; and for the presentation of difficult or unpopular truth it is invaluable. It is a flank attack on the fortifications of prejudice, its most striking virtue being its element of surprise.

The method of Jesus was distinctly inductive, as we see in all his parables. He knew that men are discoverers, and not least in the things of the spirit. He really had but one text—the greatest words ever uttered upon the earth, profounder than all philosophies and the fulfillment of every faith—"*God is love*"; but he never quoted it, much less assumed its truth as accepted. Instead, he began with facts from the life around him, and these were presented with exquisite art, converging upon his main thesis. A man giving his child bread, a farmer pulling his ox out of the pit, a father receiving a prodigal son home, a hen and her chicks, a wayside flower, a childish game, red sunsets, a wedding party, baking a loaf of bread—all life became at his touch an infinite parable of the truth that makes life worth living, investing these our days and years with epic worth and wonder. It is to be noted that he always used this method in speaking to the stranger, the doubter, and the sinner, and, since he has done more good than all of us put together, it behooves us to follow his lead.

4

John A. Broadus
1827-1895

The communication of the Word of God is central in the thinking of great preachers. In the following excerpt from **A Treatise on the Preparation and Delivery of Sermons,** * *John A. Broadus defines a text and indicates the advantages of having a biblical text for a sermon. The chapter concludes with a discussion on the selection of a text.*

——— —— —— ——

1. Meaning of the Term

The word *text* is derived from the Latin *texere*, to weave; which figuratively came to signify to put together, to construct, and hence to compose, to express thought in continuous speech or writing. The noun *textus* thus denotes the product of weaving, the web, the fabric, and so in literary usage the fabric of one's thinking, continuous composition, written or, in later times, printed. The practice arose of reading the continuous narrative or discussion of some author and adding comments, chiefly explanatory; or of taking the author's own writing and making notes at the sides or bottom of the page. Thus the author's own work came to be called the *text*, that is, the continuous, connected composition as distinguished from the fragmentary notes and comments of the editor or speaker.

* John A. Broadus, *A Treatise on the Preparation and Delivery of Sermons* (New York: Hodder and Stoughton, 1898), pp. 19-23.

This use of the word still survives, as when we speak of the text of ancient authors or others, meaning their own original composition; and *text-criticism* is the science of determining what was their exact language. So in school usage a *text-book* is so called because it is the work of the author studied, to whose continuous discussion the teacher adds notes or comments in questioning or explaining in the class. Now, early preaching was of the nature of familiar running commentary on the connected train of thought, or *text*, of Scripture, which was so named to distinguish it from the preacher's comment or exposition. As the practice grew of lengthening the comments into an orderly discourse, and of shortening the passage of Scripture expounded, the word *text* has come to mean the portion of Scripture chosen as the suggestion or foundation for a sermon.

The history of the word, like that of *homiletics*, points back to the fact, which is also well known otherwise, that preaching was originally expository. The early Christian preachers commonly spoke upon passages of considerable length, and occupied themselves largely with exposition. Frequently, however, as was natural, they would find a brief passage so fruitful as to confine themselves to it. Usage tended more and more toward the preference of short texts. In England in the seventeenth century, it was not uncommon to make many sermons on some brief passage. Thus John Howe has fourteen sermons on a part of Romans 8:24, "We are saved by hope"; seventeen on I John 4:20; and eighteen on John 3:6. The object was to make a complete discussion of some great topic, and to bind all the discourses into a whole by connecting all with the same text. But this practice conflicted with the natural love of variety. It is usually better to make a series appear such by the manifest relation of the subjects, and to choose for each discourse a separate text, which presents the particular subject or view there discussed. This is at present the common practice, it being a somewhat rare thing now to preach more than one sermon on the same brief text. There is also a tendency at present to return to the more frequent use of long texts.

2. Advantages of Having a Text

Taking a text is an old and well established custom from which there seems to be no good reason for departing; especially as the change would be sure to prove distasteful or even painful to many worthy and devout hearers of preaching. Moreover, the custom is founded in excellent reason, and has marked advantages.

It is manifest that to take a text gives a tone of sacredness to the discourse. But more than this is true. The primary idea is that the discourse is a development of the text, an explanation, illustration, application of its teachings. Our business is to teach God's word. And although we may often discuss subjects, and aspects of subjects, which are not presented in precisely that form by any passage of Scripture, yet the fundamental conception should be habitually retained, that we are about to set forth what the text contains. When circumstances determine the subject to be treated, and we have to look for a text, one can almost always be found which will have some real, though it be a general relation to the subject. If there be rare cases in which it is otherwise, it will then be better to have no text than one with which the subject has only a fanciful or forced connection.

There are several advantages in regularly taking a text. (1) It constantly recalls the fact just mentioned, that our undertaking is not to guide the people by our own wisdom, but to impart to them the teachings of God in his Word. This fact enables us to speak with confidence, and leads the people to recognize the authority of what we say. (2) If the text is well chosen, it awakens interest at the outset. (3) It often aids the hearer in remembering the train of thought, having this effect wherever the sermon is really evolved from the text. (4) It affords opportunity of explaining and impressing some passage of Scripture. (5) It tends to prevent our wandering utterly away from Scriptural topics and views. (6) Greater variety will be gained than if the mind were left altogether to the suggestion of circumstances, for then it will often fall back into its old ruts; and this variety is attained just in proportion as one restricts himself to the specific thought of each particular text.

Objections to the use of texts have commonly arisen from one of two or three causes. The grievous laxity in the interpretation of texts which has so widely prevailed, leads some men to regard the employment of them as wrong or useless. This is the old story—the abuse of a thing causing men to question the propriety of its use. Again, persons who have little or no true reverence for Scripture, or appreciation of its riches, speak of the text as a restriction upon freedom of thought and flow of eloquence. Thus Voltaire: "It were to be wished that Bourdaloue in banishing from the pulpit the bad taste which disgraced it, had also banished the custom of preaching on a text. Indeed, to speak long on a quotation of a line or two, to exhaust one's self in subjecting a whole discourse to the control of this line, seems a trifling labor, little worthy of the dignity of the ministry. The text becomes a sort of motto, or rather enigma, which the discourse develops." It seems plain that this sneer arose partly from the torturing interpretation so often witnessed, and chiefly from the critic's want of reverence for the Bible, and ignorance of the preacher's true relation to the Bible. And perhaps, as a third ground of objection to texts, some able and devout preachers, disliking expository and even textual preaching, and wishing that every sermon should be a philosophical discussion or an elaborate discourse upon a definite topic, incline to regard the custom of always taking a text as an inconvenient restriction. Such appears to have been the feeling of Vinet.

It is sometimes not unsuitable to have two texts, or even more. Thus with Hebrews 9:22, "And without shedding of blood is no remission," there might be united I John 1:7, "The blood of Jesus Christ his son cleanseth us from all sin." Or with Isaiah 6:3, "The whole earth is full of his glory," may be taken Psalm 72:19, "And let the whole earth be filled with his glory"; to angelic eyes it is so—the human mind can only pray that it may be so (cf. Hab. 2:14). Spurgeon has a sermon on the words, "I have sinned," as occuring seven times in the Bible, and gives interesting views of the different circumstances and states of mind in which they were uttered.

5

Charles H. Spurgeon
1834-1892

The sixth lecture of Spurgeon's **Lectures to My Students** *is titled "On the Choice of a Text."* * *Whereas Broadus discussed the selection of a text in terms of rules to remember, Spurgeon wrote on the selection of the text in terms of situations in which the preacher was likely to find himself. The inimitable style of Spurgeon allows the reader to empathize and develop his own rules for selecting a text.*

With regard to the sermon, we shall be most anxious, first of all, respecting the selection of the text. No one amongst us looks upon the sermon in so careless a light as to conceive that a text picked up at random will be suitable for every, or indeed, for any occasion. We are not all of Sydney Smith's mind, when he recommended a brother at a loss for a text, to preach from "Parthians, and Medes, and Elamites, and the dwellers in Mesopotamia"; as though anything would do for a sermon.

I hope we all make it a matter of very earnest and serious consideration, every week, what shall be the subjects upon which we shall address our people on the Sabbath morning and evening; for, although all Scripture is good and profitable, yet it is not all equally appropriate for every occasion. To everything there is a

* Charles H. Spurgeon, *Lectures to My Students* (1875; reprint ed., Grand Rapids: Baker Book House, 1977), pp. 84-101.

season; and everything is the better for being seasonable. A wise householder labors to give each one of the family his portion of meat in due season; he does not serve out rations indiscriminately, but suits the viands to the needs of the guests. Only a mere official, the slave of routine, the lifeless automaton of formalism, will be content to snatch at the first subject which comes to hand.

The man who plucks topics as children in the meadows gather buttercups and daisies, just as they offer themselves, may act in accordance with his position in a church into which a patron may have thrust him, and out of which the people cannot eject him, but those who profess to be called of God, and selected to their positions by the free choice of believers, will need to make fuller proof of their ministry than can be found in such carelessness. Among many gems we have to select the jewel most appropriate for the setting of the occasion. We dare not rush into the King's banquet hall with a confusion of provisions as though the entertainment were to be a vulgar scramble, but as well-mannered servitors we pause and ask the great master of the feast, "Lord, what wouldst thou have us set upon thy table this day?"

Some texts have struck us as most unhappily chosen. We wonder what Mr. Disraeli's rector did with the words, "In my flesh shall I see God," when lately preaching at a village harvest home! Exceedingly unfortunate was the funeral text for a murdered clergyman (Mr. Plow), from "So he giveth his beloved sleep." Most manifestly idiotic was he who selected "Judge not, that ye be not judged," for a sermon before the judges at an assize . . . .

It is said that a student, who it is to be hoped never emerged from the shell, preached a sermon in public, before his tutor, Dr. Philip Doddridge. Now the good man was accustomed to place himself immediately in front of the student, and look him full in the face; judge therefore of his surprise, if not indignation, when the text announced ran in these words, "Have I been so long time with you, and yet hast thou not known me, Philip?" Gentlemen, fools sometimes become students, let us hope none of that order may dishonour our Alma Mater. I pardon the man who preached before that drunken Solomon, James I of England and VI of Scotland, from James 1:6—the temptation was too great to be resisted; but let the wretch be forever execrated, if such a man ever lived, who celebrated the decease of a deacon by a tirade from, "It came to pass that the beggar died." I forgive the liar who attributed such an outrage to me, but I hope he will not try his infamous arts upon any one else . . . .

Is there any difficulty in obtaining texts? I remember, in my earlier days, reading somewhere in a volume of lectures upon Homiletics, a statement which considerably alarmed me at the time; it was something to this effect: "If any man shall find a difficulty in selecting a text, he had better at once go back to the grocer's shop, or to the plough, for he evidently has not the capacity required for a minister." Now, as such had been very frequently my cross and burden, I inquired within myself whether I should resort to some form of secular labor, and leave the ministry; but I have not done so, for I still have the conviction that, altogether condemned by the sweeping judgment of the lecturer, I follow a call to which God has manifestly set His seal.

I was so much in trouble of conscience through the aforesaid severe remark, that I asked my grandfather, who had been in the ministry some fifty years, whether he was ever perplexed in choosing his theme. He told me frankly that this had always been his greatest trouble, compared with which, preaching itself was no anxiety at all. I remember the venerable man's remark, "The difficulty is not because there are not enough texts, but because there are so many, that I am in a strait betwixt them."

Brethren, we are sometimes like the lover of choice flowers, who finds himself surrounded by all the beauties of the garden, with permission to select but one. How long he lingers between the rose and the lily, and how great the difficulty to prefer one among ten thousand blooming lovelinesses! To me still, I must confess, my text selection is a very great embarrassment—*embarras de richesses*, as the French say—an embarrassment of riches, very different from the bewilderment of poverty—the anxiety of attending to the most pressing of so many truths, all clamoring for a hearing, so many duties all needing enforcing, and so many spiritual needs of the people all demanding supply.

I confess that I frequently sit hour after hour praying and waiting for a subject, and that this is the main part of my study; much hard labor have I spent in manipulating topics, ruminating upon points of doctrine, making skeletons out of verses and then burying every bone of them in the catacombs of oblivion, sailing on and on over leagues of broken water, till I see the red lights and make sail direct to the desired haven. I believe that almost any Saturday in my life I make enough outlines of sermons, if I felt at liberty to preach them, to last me for a month, but I no more dare to use them than an honest mariner would run to shore a cargo of contraband goods. Themes flit before the mind one after another, like images passing across the photographer's lens, but until the mind is like the sensitive plate, which retains the picture, the subjects are valueless to us . . . .

"I believe in the Holy Ghost." This is one of the articles of the creed, but it is scarcely believed among professors so as to be acted on. Many ministers appear to think that they are to choose the text; they are to discover its teaching; they are to find a discourse in it. We do not think so. We are to use our own volitions, of course, as well as our understandings and affections, for we do not pretend that the Holy Ghost will compel us to preach from a text against our wills. He does not deal with us as though we were musical boxes, to be wound up and set to a certain tune; but that glorious inspirer of all truth deals with us as with rational intelligences, who are swayed by spiritual forces congruous to our nature: still, devout minds evermore desire that the choice of the text should rest with the all-wise Spirit of God, and not with their own fallible understandings, and therefore they humbly put themselves into His hand, asking Him to condescend to direct them to the portion of meat in due season which He has ordained for His people.

Gurnall says, "Ministers have no ability of their own for their work. Oh! how long may they sit tumbling their books over, and puzzling their brains, until God comes to their help, and then—as Jacob's venison—it is brought to their hand! If God drop not down His assistance, we write with a pen that hath no ink: if any one need walk dependently upon God more than another, the minister is he."

If any one enquire of me, "How shall I obtain the most proper text?" I should answer, "Cry to God for it." Harrington Evans, in his *Rules for Sermons*, lays down as the first, "Seek God in prayer for choice of a passage. Enquire why such a passage is decided upon. Let the question be fairly answered. Sometimes the answer may be such as ought to decide the mind against the choice." . . .

After prayer, we are bound with much earnestness to use fitting means for concentrating our thoughts, and directing them in the best channel. Consider the condition of your hearers. Reflect upon their spiritual state as a whole and as individuals, and prescribe the medicine adapted to the current disease, or prepare the food suitable for the prevailing necessity.

Let me caution you, however, against considering the whims of your hearers, or the peculiarities of the wealthy and influential. Do not give too much weight to the gentleman and lady who sit in the green pew, if you are so unfortunate as to possess such an abominable place of distinction in a house where all are on a level. Let the large contributor be considered by all means as much as others, and let not his spiritual infirmities be neglected; but he is not everybody, and you will grieve the Holy Spirit if you think him to be so.

Look at the poor in the aisles with equal interest, and select topics which are within their range of thought, and which may cheer them in their many sorrows. Do not suffer your heads to be turned by respect to those one-sided members of the congregation, who have a sweet tooth for one portion of the Gospel, and turn a deaf ear to other parts of truth; never go out of your way either to give them a feast or a scolding. It may be satisfactory to think that they are pleased, if they are good people, and one respects their predilections, but faithfulness demands that we should not become mere pipers to our hearers, playing such tunes as they may demand of us, but should remain as the Lord's mouth to declare all His counsels . . . .

Consider what sins appear to be most rife in the church and congregation—worldliness, covetousness, prayerlessness, wrath, pride, want of brotherly love, slander, and such like evils. Take into account, affectionately, the trials of your people, and seek for a balm for their wounds . . . .

. . . We must watch the spiritual state of our people, and if we notice that they are falling into a backsliding condition; if we fear that they are likely to be inoculated by any mischievous heresy or perverse imagining; if anything, in fact, in the whole physiological character of the church should strike our mind, we must hasten to prepare a sermon which, by God's grace, may stay the plague.

These are the indications among His hearers which the Spirit of God gives to the careful, observant pastor as to his line of action. The careful shepherd often examines his flock, and governs his mode of treatment by the state in which he finds it. He will be likely to supply one sort of food but sparingly, and another in great abundance, and medicine in its due quantity, according as his practiced judgment finds the one or the other necessary. We shall be rightly directed if we do but associate ourselves with "that great Shepherd of the sheep."

Do not, however, let us allow our preaching right home to our people to degenerate into scolding them. They call the pulpit "Cowards' Castle," and it is a very proper name for it in some respects, especially when fools mount the platform and imprudently insult their hearers by holding up their faults or infirmities to pub-

lic derision. There is a personality—an offensive, wanton, unjusti-
fiable personality—which is to be studiously avoided; it is of the
earth, earthy, and is to be condemned in unmeasured terms; while
there is another personality, wise, spiritual, heavenly, which is to
be aimed at unceasingly. The Word of God is sharper than any
two-edged sword, and therefore you can leave the Word of God to
wound and kill, and need not be yourselves cutting in phrase and
manner. God's truth is searching: leave it to search the hearts of
men without offensive additions from yourself. He is a mere
bungler in portrait painting who needs to write the name under the
picture when it is hung up in the family parlor where the person
himself is sitting. . . .

Supposing, however, that you have prayed in that little room of
yours, have wrestled hard and supplicated long, and have thought
over your people and their wants, and still you cannot meet with
the text—well, do not fret about it, nor give way to despair. If you
were about to go into a warfare at your own charges, it would be a
very miserable thing to be short of powder, and the battle so near;
but as your Captain has to provide, there is no doubt that all in
good time He will serve out the ammunition. If you trust in God,
He will not, He cannot, fail you. Continue pleading and watching,
for to the industrious student heavenly help is certain. If you had
gone up and down idly all the week, and given no heed to proper
preparation, you could not expect divine aid; but if you have done
your best, and are now waiting to know your Lord's message, your
face shall never be ashamed . . . .

. . . At New Park Street, I once passed through a very singular experience, of which witnesses are present in this room. I had passed
happily through all the early parts of divine service in the evening
of the Sabbath, and was giving out the hymn before [the] sermon. I
opened the Bible to find the text, which I had carefully studied as
the topic of discourse, when on the opposite page another passage
of Scripture sprang upon me like a lion from a thicket, with vastly
more power than I had felt when considering the text which I had
chosen.

The people were singing and I was sighing. I was in a strait betwixt two, and my mind hung as in the balances. I was naturally
desirous to run in the track which I had carefully planned, but the
other text would take no refusal, and seemed to tug at my skirts,
crying,"No, no, you must preach from me. God would have you
follow me." I deliberated within myself as to my duty, for I would
neither be fanatical or unbelieving, and at last I thought within
myself, "Well, I should like to preach the sermon which I have pre-

pared, and it is a great risk to run to strike out a new line of thought, but still as this text constrains me, it may be of the Lord, and therefore I will venture upon it, come what may."

I almost always announce my divisions very soon after the exordium, but on this occasion, contrary to my usual custom, I did not do so, for a reason which some of you may probably guess. I passed through the first head with considerable liberty, speaking perfectly extemporaneously both as to thought and word. The second point was dwelt upon with a consciousness of unusual, quiet, efficient power, but I had no idea what the third would or could be, for the text yielded no more matter just then, nor can I tell even now what I could have done had not an event occurred upon which I had never calculated.

I had brought myself into great difficulty by obeying what I thought to be a divine impulse, and I felt comparatively easy about it, believing that God would help me, and knowing that I could at least close the service should there be nothing more to be said. I had no need to deliberate, for in one moment we were in total darkness—the gas had gone out, and as the aisles were choked with people, and the place everywhere crowded, it was a great peril, but a great blessing. What was I to do then? The people were a little frightened, but I quieted them instantly by telling them not to be at all alarmed, though the gas was out, for it would soon be relighted; and as for myself, having no manuscript, I could speak as well in the dark as in the light, if they would be so good as to sit and listen. Had my discourse been ever so elaborate, it would have been absurd to have continued it, and so as my plight was, I was all the less embarrassed.

I turned at once mentally to the well-known text which speaks of the child of light walking in darkness, and the child of darkness walking in the light, and found appropriate remarks and illustrations pouring in upon me, and when the lamps were again lit, I saw before me an audience as rapt and subdued as ever a man beheld in his life. The odd thing of all was, that some few church meetings afterwards, two persons came forward to make confession of their faith, who professed to have been converted that evening; but the first owed her conversion to the former part of the discourse, which was on the new text that came to me, and the other traced his awakening to the latter part, which was occasioned by the sudden darkness. Thus, you see, Providence befriended me. I cast myself upon God, and His arrangements quenched the light at the proper time for me . . . .

As a further assistance to a poor stranded preacher, who cannot launch his mind for want of a wave or two of thought, I recommend him in such case, to turn again and again to the Word of God itself, and read a chapter, and ponder over its verses one by one; or let him select a single verse, and get his mind fully exercised upon it. It may be that he will not find his text in the verse or chapter which he reads, but the right word will come to him through his mind being actively engaged upon holy subjects. According to the relation of thoughts to each other, one thought will suggest another, and another, until a long procession will have passed before the mind, out of which one or other will be the predestinated theme.

Read also good suggestive books, and get your mind aroused by them. If men wish to get water out of a pump which has not been lately used, they first pour water down, and then the pump works. Reach down [to] one of the Puritans, and thoroughly study the work, and speedily you will find yourself like a bird on the wing, mentally active and full of motion.

By way of precaution, however, let me remark that we ought to be always in training for text-getting and sermon-making. We should constantly preserve the holy activity of our minds. Woe unto the minister who dares to waste an hour. Read John Foster's *Essay on the Improvement of Time*, and resolve never to lose a second of it. A man who goes up and down from Monday morning till Saturday night, and indolently dreams that he is to have his text sent down by an angelic messenger in the last hour or two of the week, tempts God, and deserves to stand speechless on the Sabbath. We have no leisure as ministers; we are never off duty, but are on our watchtowers day and night.

Students, I tell you solemnly, nothing will excuse you from the most rigid economy of time; it is at your peril that you trifle with it. The leaf of your ministry will soon wither unless, like the blessed man in the first Psalm you meditate in the law of the Lord both day and night. I am most anxious that you should not throw away time in religious dissipation, or in gossiping and frivolous talk. Beware of running about from this meeting to that, listening to mere twaddle, and contributing your share to the general blowing up of windbags. A man great at tea-drinkings, evening parties, and Sunday school excursions, is generally little everywhere else. Your pulpit preparations are your first business, and if you neglect these, you will bring no credit upon yourself or your office. Bees are making honey from morning till night, and we should be always gathering stores for our people. I have no belief in that ministry which ignores laborious preparation . . . .

. . . Very much of the preacher's power will lie in his whole soul being in accord with the subject, and I should be afraid to appoint a subject for a certain date lest, when the time come, I should not be in the key for it. Besides, it is not easy to see how a man can exhibit dependence upon the guidance of the Spirit of God, when he has already prescribed his own route. Perhaps you will say, "That is a singular objection, for why not rely upon Him for twenty weeks as well as for one." True, but we have never had a promise to warrant such faith. God promises us grace according to our days, but He says nothing of endowing us with a reserve fund for the future.

> Day by day the manna fell;
> Oh, to learn this lesson well!

Even so will our sermons come to us, fresh from heaven, when required. I am jealous of anything which should hinder your daily dependence upon the Holy Spirit, and therefore I register the opinion already given. To you, my younger brethren, I feel safe in saying with authority: leave ambitious attempts at elaborate series of discourses to older and abler men. We have but a small share of mental gold and silver, let us invest our little capital in useful goods which will obtain a ready market, and leave the wealthier merchants to deal in more expensive and cumbrous articles. We know not what a day may bring forth—let us wait for daily teaching, and do nothing which might preclude us from using those materials which Providence may today or tomorrow cast in our way.

Perhaps you will ask whether you should preach from texts which persons select for you, and request you to preach upon. My answer would be, as a rule, never; and if there must be exceptions let them be few. Let me remind you that you do not keep a shop to which customers may come and give their orders. When a friend suggests a topic, think it over, and consider whether it be appropriate, and see whether it comes to you with power. Receive the request courteously, as you are in duty bound to do as a gentleman and a Christian; but if the Lord whom you serve does not cast His light upon the text, do not preach from it, let who may persuade you.

6
F. B. Meyer
1847-1929

As F. B. Meyer's style matured, he found the best style of preaching for him was expository preaching which related the Bible to his congregation. His style is described in **Expository Preaching: Plans and Methods.** *Expository preaching has come to have several shades of meaning. For Meyer expository preaching involved not only the exposition of a biblical text but also the application of the text to the needs of his congregation.*

Meyer began preaching when he was sixteen years old. His fame spread especially after he became pastor of Christ Church, Westminster Bridge Road, Lambeth, in 1888. Early in his ministry he developed the habit of diligent study in preparation for preaching. During intensive study the sermon would develop in his mind. His natural gift for eloquence combined with hard work and his deeply spiritual personal life made him a pulpit giant.

The following excerpt is from chapter two of **Expository Preaching: Plans and Methods.** *The chapter is titled "Expository Preaching—What It Is."* *

There are many kinds of preaching, and he is the wise and successful man who knows how to vary them. As the husbandman rotates his crops, and adopts many methods to extract the utmost re-

---

* F. B. Meyer, *Expository Preaching: Plans and Methods* (1913; reprint ed., Grand Rapids: Baker Book House, 1974), pp. 29-37.

sponse from the soil, so in the spiritual realm "the vetches are beaten out with a staff and the cummin with a rod" (Isa. 38:23).

Our Lord's first sermon was an example of the *topical* method. He read out His text, interpreted it, drew out the doctrine of it, illustrated it by Scripture examples, and was proceeding to apply it, when He was interrupted by the mad fury of His audience. *Biographical* preaching has found a chief exponent in our day in the masterly analysis of character given by Dr. Whyte, of Edinburgh, laying hold of the salient features and characteristics, and enforcing them for imitation or warning. *Doctrinal* preaching used to be more in vogue than it is, and found noble examples especially in the Scotch pulpits. It is a great treat to hear a sermon that gathers together various portions of Scripture and builds on their collation and comparison some sublime aspect of Divine truth, much as a scientist would from a number of isolated instances deduce the great natural law which co-ordinates them. It is well, sometimes, to have recourse to the hortatory method, in which the preacher exhorts his congregation to some neglected duty, to repent, to administer their property with more punctilious care for the claims of God, or to undertake some fresh field of activity. But among all these *expository* preaching should have a very conspicuous place. It should be the standing dish; nay, it is the table on which all the dishes are placed. From the point of view of this paper there is no reason why each of the foregoing should not find a place in the scheme of expository discourse.

Probably the ideal is that followed by the late Dr. W. M. Taylor, of New York, who said: "My own practice has been, for many years, to give up one of the services of each Lord's Day to the systematic exposition of some book of Scripture, leaving the other free for the presentation of such subjects as may be suggested by the occurrences of the times or the circumstances of my people. This division I have felt to be not only very convenient, but also extremely serviceable."

It is necessary to indicate the mistakes that have been made in regard to the nature of the kind of preaching for which we plead— mistakes which have brought it into disrepute in many quarters. We do not mean, for instance, that the preacher should take a longer or shorter chapter and preface his remarks by saying, "Dear brethren, I propose to make a few remarks on this portion of Scripture," and so proceed to utter a few pious platitudes about the successive verses. This is milk and water with a vengeance, especially water, and that not hot. If the man of the world were to drop into such a parody of preaching, he might fairly go off after the first five minutes, thinking that religion might do well enough for women and children, but had nothing for him. A preacher of that sort, giving a lecture on the Minor Prophets, came finally to the Book of Amos. "We have now come to Amos," he said; "what shall we do with him?" A man sitting in the rear of the house said, loud enough to be heard by his neighbours, "He can have my seat, for I'm going home." This is one great advantage in open-air preaching; the audience departs unless there is enough honey to attract and keep the bees.

Still less, by expository preaching, do we mean that the preacher should give an exhaustive and exhausting digest of all the commentaries to which he has access. Congregations want results, and not the process by which they are acquired. It is necessary, of course, that the expository preacher should regard his paragraph or chapter under all the varying lights flashed on it from different minds, but there is no need to marshal all these venerable and learned men in the pulpit and give them to opportunity of demolishing one another. When people want food they are impatient with learned discussions as to the most wholesome dietary.

It is also a mistaken view of expository preaching which leads the minister to dwell minutely and particularly on every point in the Scripture with which he is dealing. Pre-Raphaelite painting has its merits, but in these hurrying days it is necessary to concentrate the mind on some one striking figure or conception. Men will not stop to count the number of petals in a daisy.

It is also possible, when expository preaching is rightly practised, to combine the didactic with the passionate, teaching with intensity, and explanation with appeal. John Knox was a prince among expositors. Indeed, it is to him that Scotland owes the custom still observed by the majority of its ministers, of devoting at least one of their discourses on each Lord's Day to the regular and consecutive exposition of some book of Scripture. In the First Book of Discipline, which was drawn up mainly by him, we have the following direction: "We think it most expedient that the Scriptures be read in order—that is, that some one book of the Old and the New Testaments be begun, and orderly read to the end. And the same *we judge of preaching, where the minister for the most part remaineth in one place*; for this skipping and divagation from place to place, be it in reading or be it in preaching, we judge not so profitable to edify the church." But that exposition in his hands was no languid, lifeless or scholastic explanation of the passage under consideration is clear from this graphic description of him in his last days by James Melville: "I heard him teach the prophecies of Daniel that summer and the winter following. In the opening of his text he was moderate for the space of half an hour; but when he entered on the application he made me so to shiver (*Scottice*, 'grue') and tremble that I could not hold my pen to write. He was very weak, but before he had done with his sermon he was so active and vigorous that it seemed as if he would knock the pulpit in pieces (*Scottice*, 'ding the pulpit in blads') and fly out of it." Wherever he laboured, his method was the same. The English Ambassador at the Court of Scotland described what he had himself seen, when he wrote to Cecil: "I assure you the voice of one man is able in an hour to put more life in us than six hundred trumpets blustering in our ears."

We are now able, in the light of these distinctions, to define expository preaching as *the consecutive treatment of some book or extended portion of Scripture* on which the preacher has concentrated head and heart, brain and brawn, over which he has thought and wept and prayed, until it has yielded up its inner secret, and the spirit of it has passed into his spirit. That passion which we were just remarking in John Knox revealed itself in Rutherford and Chalmers, in Cairns and Caird. It is not an artifice nor a trick; it is probably the possession of a man's nature by the Spirit which hides in true and sacred words, as sparks lie hid in flint. It is thus that the spirit of nature is concealed from all save her wooers, who wait patiently until she coyly drops her veil and shows her face. The highest point of sermon-utterance is when a preacher is "possessed," and certainly, in the judgment of the writer, such possession comes oftenest and easiest to a man who has lived, slept, walked and eaten in fellowship with a passage for the best part of a week.

But let us consider more particularly the method adopted by the expository preacher. We will suppose that he has been led to choose either the Book of Exodus or the Epistle to the Hebrews. He will perhaps have made his selection for the coming autumn and winter before he starts on his summer vacation. With all his other preparations for golf, or fishing, or camping out, he takes a handy pocket copy of the chosen Scripture. On the moor or in the hammock, within sound of the break of the waves or of the crunching of glaciers, he reads again and again, until the central lesson, the *motif*, begins to reveal itself. The next step is to roughly divide the matter under some general divisions, which will be broken up ultimately into smaller and yet smaller ones, the one condition being that each paragraph or chapter shall contain one complete thought.

For instance, I am now at work with the Book of Exodus. Sometimes a few verses give me concisely and completely all that is needed for an effective sermon; as for example, 2:23-25 or 6:2-9. But at another time the whole chapter must be compressed into one discourse, as chapter 18, which could not be subdivided without serious detriment to the symmetry and force of the lesson it contains. The Epistle to the Hebrews is one of the easiest books in the Bible for division and subdivision. The least intelligent after reading it once or twice can see the natural compartments of this wonderful treatise; but the pieces of separate mosaic combine in a picture to which each is necessary, and none is complete without the rest. This earliest process of parcelling out the rich tract of land before us is one of the most fascinating experiments of the preacher's life; and he contrives, as far as possible, that in every portion there should be a tiny bit of mountain moorland with its heather, some granite rocks, some foothills, corn for the gleaners, and flowers for the children.

When one has made one's own divisions it is time to turn to see what others have done in the same directions. Often what seemed to be the best and most original of your findings will have been anticipated. Not unfrequently you will alight on the divisions of a Maclaren or a Storrs so perfect that you cannot but substitute it for your own. Generally the collision of another man's brain with yours will strike out some fresh conception, which carries the likeness of the father and mother of its parentage.

When this is settled a great deal is settled. The land has been divided among the tribes, and the tribes into families, and the families into individual plots. It only remains to discover the pivot sentence in the next group of verses which you are proposing to treat. That phrase "pivot sentence" is absolutely important. There is in each paragraph one sentence on which it resolves, or a point on which it impinges, like the rocking stones left by the glacier period in balance, as though angels had been playing at a pastime of herculean feats.

It is a mistake for the preacher to read out a whole long paragraph as the text of his sermon. Should he do so, the ordinary mind wearily anticipates a long discourse, and all the boys and girls, who are expected to repeat or write out the text as a Sunday task, wince. The text should be appetising, like the liquors which, I am told, are taken by *bon-vivants* before their meals. It should be terse and crisp, bright and short, easily remembered and quotable. In every chapter and paragraph there is one such. In that mentioned from the Book of Exodus, the chord or keynote is struck in "Be thou for the people God-ward." If the preacher announces this as his text, attention is awakened and interest excited. People wonder what he will make of it; and the stranger within the gates will not suppose that the sermon is one of a series.

It is a profound mistake for the expository preacher to spend any time in recapitulation. He ought never to utter the phrase, "As I was saying last Sunday." There is no need for it, and it only conveys an immediate sense of the incompleteness of the present address. Each sermon should be complete in itself and should not require to be propped up against another to make it stand. Equally unsuitable is it to talk of what you have to say next Sunday, unless under special circumstances, such as the immensity of the theme, of which you could only give one aspect. But these tricks for catching audiences are not the best. Give the people something worth coming for, and they will come. At the same time it is undeniable that young regular hearers will become interested as soon as they see that their pastor is pursuing a regular line of study and teaching, and will make every endeavour not to miss one link in the chain of thought.

When the pivot-text is chosen it is desirable, so far as possible, to weave into the structure of the sermon all the main points of the surrounding paragraph. There is no absolute law in the matter except one's own sense of the fitness of things. Just as all the objects in the field of vision focus in the lens of the eye, and finally in the minute filament of the optic nerve, so the thoughts, images and suggestions of the context should pass through the chosen motto to the heart of the people.

The main burden of all our preaching, as we have seen, must be Jesus Christ, and the expositor questions often how much of Christ there is present and how he can make Him known. He remembers that the Lord told His critics that Moses wrote of Him (John 5:46) and that He interpreted to the two who walked to Emmaus in *all* the Scriptures the things concerning Himself (Luke 25:27). Did not the angel that showed the beloved apostle the crowding glories of the unseen assure him that the testimony of Jesus was the spirit of prophecy? (Rev. 19:10).

Expository preachers have the two experiences set forth in our Lord's parables. Sometimes when they start on the preparation of their sermon, seeking the goodly pearls of truth, they suddenly come on one of great price, which so excels the others that they lose sight of all the rest and sell all for the excellency of the knowledge of Christ Jesus their Lord. The paragraph becomes a veritable transfiguration mountain, on which they lose sight of even Moses and Elijah and see no man but Jesus only. At other times they resemble the ploughman represented in the alternate parable, who was ploughing over a hard and rather uninteresting field and suddenly heard his plough clink against metal. Immediately he dropped the ploughtail and ran forward to see what he had struck. He had alighted on a strong metal chest containing the savings of a life, which the owner had buried for safety, but had died suddenly without giving the clue of its whereabouts to his children. Many a track of Scripture, when we first read it over, seems as though it were hardly worth considering, and then the hidden Christ is suddenly discovered; and to have found Him is to have come on a mine of treasure from which the whole congregation will be enriched on the following Lord's Day.

It was said of Philip Henry that he did not shoot the arrow of the Word *over the heads* of his audience in affected rhetoric, nor *under their feet* by homely expressions, but *to their hearts* in close and lively application. Such should be our aim in dealing with any part of God's Word; we must apply it to each individual in the audience. Each bearer must be as one who stands on the seashore on a moonlight night. The waves of Scriptural teaching must break at his feet, and the path of light over the waters must come to where he stands. We must preach *to* the people as well as before them. It has been well said that a good sermon should resemble a good portrait, in looking directly at each in the room and saying, I have a message for thee. It is not enough to expatiate lucidly or eloquently on a passage of Scripture; we must show each person that it has a message for him, that it belongs to him, that he must heed it and obey.

7

Halford E. Luccock
1885-1960

*In 1928 Halford E. Luccock was appointed Professor of Homiletics at the Yale Divinity School. During his twenty-five years at Yale, Luccock made his greatest contributions to homiletics, including the publication of his most popular book, **In the Minister's Workshop**. He also delivered the 1953 Lyman Beecher Lectures on Preaching, which were published under the title, **Communicating the Gospel**.*

*Luccock enjoyed his work as both a preacher and a teacher of preaching. The joy he felt is obvious in his writings. Among the several contributions Luccock made to homiletics was his approach to preaching as an art form. The excerpt which follows is from chapter four of **In the Minister's Workshop**.* In this book, Luccock expounds his views on topics in preaching such as the spiritual commitment of the preacher, the need for biblical study, and how to communicate to a contemporary congregation.*

An Art Is a Band of Music

Only a small part of the field of the preacher's craftsmanship has been traveled over when we become sharply aware of the pitfalls of a distorted preoccupation with any technique. Personal and profes-

* Halford E. Luccock, *In the Minister's Workshop* (1944; reprint ed., Grand Rapids: Baker Book House, 1977), pp. 31-36.

sional calamity impends when a means becomes an end. Yet we
dare not forget that the end depends on the means. A consideration
of ends without attention to means is pure sentimentalism.

What often fails to receive attention at anything like its true
value is the recognition of what a deep and lifelong interest in the
technical side of his art will do for a preacher, in the sustaining of
enthusiasm and vivacity, in preventing the calamity which has
overtaken so many preachers when the toil of sermon making becomes a chore, "stale as the remainder biscuit after a voyage."

Robert Louis Stevenson well expressed this preserving function of
an interest in art: "An art is a band of music." Who ever proved
that up to the hilt more than he? It was a resource that even a lifetime of fighting hemorrhages could not deplete. The band of music
still played in the last days; and it was not a death march when, an
exile in the South Pacific, his voice completely gone, he learned the
deaf-and-dumb alphabet so that he could dictate a last novel to
Isobel Strong. It is right at that point of a workman's joy in his job
that one of the most significant dividing lines runs between ministers. We read in the Book of Acts of Paul's meeting a certain group
who had never heard of the Holy Ghost. There is a true parallel in
the company of preachers who have never so much as heard of
another holy spirit, the thing that keeps a true maker of any sort—
artist, musician, sculptor, architect, skilled artisan—renewed in the
inward man—an interest in the craft itself, in the overcoming of
the particular obstacles, in the creation of beauty and of the form
that fulfills the function. That will carry a man through the inevitably recurring low tides of the spirit when even the sense of the
presence of God recedes.

An art is a band of music. Without its accompaniment on the
professional march many a man in the pulpit moves with the
heavy, mechanical trudge of Kipling's soldier—"Boots—boots—
boots—boots—movin' up an' down again."

Without a truly re-creating interest in the technique of creation
the minister may be haunted with a dire apparition following him:
"I have a little shadow that goes in and out with me"—the shadow
of next Sunday's sermon. He may even feel,

> And my soul from out that shadow
> . . . .
> Shall be lifted—nevermore!

We are assured, "Ye shall know the truth, and the truth shall make
you free." It is also true that a serious interest in the practice of art,

restlessly experimenting to find a better medium and method, will make a preacher free—free from a fatal ennui that can strike at the mind and soul.

That is the glory of teaching, found—not rarely, thank God, but often—in a teacher whose interest in his professional task is a life preserver of the spirit, whose reward is not in any prestige or money but in the thing in itself—the miracle of communication. Bliss Perry has given a memorable picture of a great teacher trans-figured by that absorbing interest, Louis Agassiz: "Louis Agassiz, whose gift for research was doubted by no one, but who was never happier than when he was standing in front of a blackboard in a crossroads schoolhouse before an audience of farmers, armed with a clamshell and a piece of chalk." Shining armor—a clamshell and a piece of chalk! In that picture change the country schoolhouse to a country church, leave the audience of farmers just the same, substitute a Bible for the clamshell—and you have the preacher, sustained not by any insignificant paraphernalia of his profession but by the thing in itself.

For it is only through a maker's joy that one comes into a strange mystery of preaching: its excitement in the effort of accomplishing an intricate task. The more lethargic and unpromising the au-dience, the greater the excitement of the preacher. It is just "the given" with which he has to deal. A sermon is like a wrestling match, or rather two wrestling matches, first with an idea and then with an audience, with the absorbed tenseness of those first mo-ments which will determine whether one can get an effective hold on idea or on people.

There is a further mystery about preaching, a providence of God without which we would all droop and faint, in that blessed illu-sion that if we do a creditable job one time out of twenty, we are buoyed up by the feeling that this one achievement is our true form. A merciful cloud blots out the nineteen misfires. That same joyous illusion operates notably in golf. A man may go around the course with a sum total of a hundred more-or-less dub shots. And then comes the miracle—a clean, hard drive which sends the ball singing on its flight, making a celestial music to which only a golfer's ear is attuned. Then he lifts his head, squares his shoulders, feels the equivalent of a *Te Deum*, and says, "Now I am hitting my stride. That is my true form!" And the memory of that one shot puts to flight any painful recollection of the ninety and nine hooks and slices and divot digging. That sustaining mystery of preach-ing—call it illusion if you will—is a special grace by which the preacher is enabled to obey the command, "Be not weary in well doing." But it is present only when one has a craftsman's interest in his tools and tasks.

This preserving interest in an increasing skill is not at all unrelated to the content of the message. It is inseparable from a real feeling of the momentousness of the message. Henry James put this concisely in his dogma that "what is merely stated is never really presented." That ought never to be absent from a minister's mind and conscience. If the difference between those two verbs "stated" and "presented" could be clearly seen and strongly felt, the persuasive power of ten thousand pulpits would be vastly increased in effectiveness. It is so easy to "state"; it is so hard to "present." Merely stating a truth, from "Honesty is the best policy" all the way up or down the scale of acknowledged axioms, can be done in one's sleep, and is frequently so done. The soporific qualities of merely "stating" surpass those of laudanum. But to *present* a truth, a persuasion, a warning, or an appeal; to sharpen its form so that it can etch itself on the mind; to give it the mobility of surprise, so that it gets past the guards which the minds of a congregation raise; to breathe into words the very breath of life so that they become a living soul—that is so difficult as to deserve the toil of years. One of the frankest personal revelations of the cost and reward of a command of words is that of J. B. Priestley in his filling in of the phrase "engrossed by an art." "The difference between us," he writes, referring to some early fellow practitioners of writing,

was not in ability, but in the fact that while at heart they did not really much care about authorship, but merely toyed with the fascinating idea of it, I cared like blazes. And I suspect that in any form of art, it is this caring like blazes, while you are still young, that counts. Because you care and the dream never fades, other things, looking like those gifts of the gods, are added unto you. The very passion of the heart draws power. In some mysterious fashion, I suspect, you orientate your being so that such gifts as observation, invention and imagination are pulled your way. This explains why certain actors, from the Irving of yesterday to the Laughton of to-day, who begin with the gravest natural disadvantages, with obvious weaknesses of appearance, gait, voice, have ended as masters of their art. A mere desire for the rewards, no matter how constant and burning that desire may be, will not do the trick. You have to be fascinated from the first by the art itself, engrossed and spellbound, and not simply dazzled by the deceptively superior life of its successful practitioners. In this matter you have, in short, to be pure in heart before you can be blessed.

The goal, the effective presentation of a true word which can set men on their feet, even when its setting is of the simplest, is so great as to deserve any extent of discipline and sacrifice. That goal is movingly pictured in David Morton's conception of how great a thing a poem may be; it applies as truly to a sermon:

> To make a small sound
> In a large place,
> So that, for miles around,
> It being of such grace,
>
> All other sound is stilled,
> Though a moment only,
> And all the air is filled
> With the grave and lonely
>
> Listening to a word
> Wherein is drowned
> All else, and nothing heard
> Save this small sound.

All of this, of course, compels the enlargement and deepening of that word "craft" as commonly used. It must include the "spirit in which" as well as "the means by which" a given article is produced. That was true of skilled handworkers, silversmiths, pottery makers—of many artisans. It is supremely true of the artisan of the words of life.

Now to conclude this chapter on a very practical level. The consideration to follow does not move on the heights of prophecy, but it grazes closely a matter of great concern to every preacher—his possible length of service in a parish. One lengendary figure of literature ought to be well remembered by every preacher. She is Scheherazade, the ingenious raconteur who told the stories which make up the *Arabian Nights.* The origin of the stories is traced to the pleasant custom of a caliph who married many brides successively and always beheaded them the next morning. Finally he married Scheherazade, who was very evidently much more than a "glamour girl." She had wit and resourcefulness. She told her lord and temporary husband on her wedding night a story of such enthralling interest and suspense that the execution was postponed for a day that the caliph might learn "what happened next." The next installment was equally gripping and unfinished. So the execution was again deferred, to be followed by a thousand and one nights of storytelling. A life preserved by the sheer interest of a story! That is not a cynical picture of the situation of the Protestant minister. His life is prolonged in a parish, the writ of execution is stayed by the pulpit-supply committee, the overhanging sword is held back, by the sheer interest of the preacher's story in the pulpit. Character, sympathy, faithfulness all count. But in so many churches the execution, in the form of a desire for a new minister, is postponed through the minister's skill as a Scheherazade, the sustaining of the desire to listen again. On the other hand, many a pulpit committee, growing tired of a twice-told tale, stirred to no expectation by the plot of the story, has ordered the execution at dawn.

Van Wyck Brooks has put this true state of affairs into words of personal confession: "Every day I begin my work with the same old feeling, that I am on trial for my life and will probably not be acquitted." The minister is truly on trial for his life, and acquittal will come partly through a retention and increase of skilled workmanship. Let him who in jaunty complacency has no fears aroused by the story of Scheherazade remember the word of Joseph Conrad, "The stuff that comes easy is dull reading." And we may add an ecclesiastical postscript, "dull hearing."

One of the priceless equipments of a preacher is a limp, of the sort that Jacob got from wrestling with an angel. Toiling at a craft with intensity is wrestling with an angel of the Lord.

PART THREE
Essential Qualities for Effective Preaching

1

James Stuart Stewart
1896-

*This second excerpt from **Heralds of God** is titled "The Preacher's Technique."* It illustrates Stewart's unique contribution to preaching, that of speaking clearly and with appeal.*

——— — ———

It may be well at this point to say something on the question of language. Two pitfalls against which I have already warned you are professionalism of vocabulary or pulpit jargon, and the temptations of the purple passage: on these nothing further need be said. Let me rather go on to stress one great positive rule which ought to determine your choice of language throughout: Be simple and direct. "People think," exclaimed Matthew Arnold, "that I can teach them style. What stuff it all is! Have something to say, and say it as clearly as you can. That is the only secret of style." Surely Arnold was right. Every man at Pentecost heard the Gospel, we are told, in his own tongue; and that is the basic condition of effective preaching still. Have something to say, and when you are saying it avoid periphrasis and over-elaboration: say it as clearly as you can. Dr. L. P. Jacks maintains that "two lines of Wordsworth—

> But she is in her grave, and, oh,
> The difference to me!

are a more adequate expression of human grief than all the funeral

* James S. Stewart, *Heralds of God* (1946; reprint ed., Grand Rapids: Baker Book House, 1972), pp. 149-53.

sermons ever preached." It is simple directness, not literary embellishment, that moves the hearts of men.

Let us hark back, by way of contrast, to St. Paul's Cathedral at Christmastide 1624, and listen to this trumpet-toned, tremendous utterance of John Donne. He is speaking of the Psalmist's word, "I will sing of mercy and judgment." "If some King of the earth," cries Donne, "have so large an extent of Dominion, in North, and South, as that he hath Winter and Summer together in his Dominions, so large an extent East and West, as that he hath day and night together in his Dominions, much more hath God mercy and judgment together; He brought light out of darknesse, not out of a lesser light; He can bring thy Summer out of Winter, though thou have no Spring; though in the wayes of fortune, or understanding, or conscience, thou have been benighted till now, wintred and frosen, clouded and eclipsed, damped and benumbed, smothered and stupified till now, now God comes to thee, not as in the dawning of the day, not as in the bud of the spring, but as the Sun at noon to illustrate all shadowes, as the sheaves in harvest, to fill all penuries, all occasions invite His mercies, and all times are His seasons." That is magnificent—but try modelling your sermon language upon it, and the result is likely to be disastrous. Or take this, from a preacher of a very different kind, Talmage of Brooklyn. He has just quoted the railing cry of the impenitent malefactor at Calvary, "If Thou be the Son of God"—and he goes on, "If? Was there any if about it? Tell me, thou star, that in robe of life didst run to point out His birthplace. Tell me, thou sea, that didst put thy hand over thy lip when He bid thee be still. Tell me, ye dead, who got up to see Him die. Tell me, thou sun in mid-heaven, who for Him didst pull down over thy face the veil of darkness. Tell me, ye lepers, who were cleansed, ye dead, who were raised. Is He the Son of God? Aye, aye! responds the universe. The flowers breathe it—the stars chime it—the redeemed celebrate it—the angels rise up on their thrones to announce it. And yet on that miserable malefactor's 'if' millions shall be wrecked for all eternity." That, again, is great preaching: and you, too, may have—please God, will often have—those moments when language, winged with the emotion of a mighty theme, soars aloft in genuine eloquence. But artificial eloquence, like sham emotion, is a dreadful thing. Learn to prune your language. Reject every expression that is merely florid and ostentatious. Prefer simple and even homely words to those that are abstract and difficult, direct and pointed speech to involved circuitous sentences. Not that you need be arid and prosaic: but you must be lucid. Do not be like the writers Quiller-Couch describes, "perpetually shuffling around in the fog and cotton-wool of abstract terms." Canon Liddon was writing a letter to a friend one dark Christmas from Amen Court. "London is just now," he wrote, "buried under a dense fog. This is commonly attributed to Dr. Westcott having opened his study-window at Westminster." That, of course, was quite unfair. But clarity is a consummation so devoutly to be wished that you must be ready to sacrifice almost anything to achieve it.

In thus urging upon you the necessity of lucid and simple language, I am certainly not suggesting that the best preaching is that which makes a minimum demand upon the hearers for mental exertion and hard thinking. Simplicity is a very different thing from shallowness; and if it is bad to preach over people's heads, not to preach to their heads at all is worse. I trust that to your dying day you will "preach the simple Gospel," but it is well to remember that there is nothing which so stretches men's mental horizons as God's revelation in Christ. It was a true insight that led the apostle to declare, "The world by wisdom knew not God": but it is a deplorable attitude which would divorce evangelism from the duty of disciplined thought. There is a type of preaching which apparently regards it as more important to generate heat than to supply light: sermons devoid of any element of positive teaching, compounded of anecdotes, appeals and homiletical "gush," an affront to any decent man's intelligence, "full of sound and fury, signifying nothing." Some preachers have the fixed idea that the way to reach the human heart is to by-pass the human understanding. It is emphatically mistaken strategy. *Das Denken ist auch Gottesdienst*; and nothing could be more tedious than the preaching which is all uplift and exhortation with no food to feed the mind. Resolve, then, that your pulpit work shall represent not only your truest fervour but also your best thought. Your congregation deserves it, and will welcome it. But even with the deep and difficult themes that tax the mind—with these, indeed, most of all—the rule applies: Be clear, be direct. Rabbi Duncan was discussing with a friend one day the merits and demerits of a certain essay. "Is it not deep?" his friend inquired admiringly. "No," came the blunt expressive answer, "not deep, but drumlie!"

2
Joseph Parker
1830-1902

Joseph Parker was a man who never lacked self-confidence. His contemporaries were C. H. Spurgeon, F. B. Meyer, and Alexander MacLaren. Despite this stiff competition for the limelight, Parker received a good deal of public attention.

Parker's fame began with a call in 1869 to pastor the Poultry Church in London. With typical self-assurance he accepted the call on the condition that the church immediately begin construction of a larger building to hold the crowds he would soon be commanding. The result was the City Temple of London.

Parker enjoyed his duties as preacher and administrator of the church but disliked other pastoral roles, especially visitation. His distaste for "pastoral calls" is expressed in this excerpt on "Earnestness," which is chapter two of **Ad Clerum: Advices to a Young Preacher.** * *As did Spurgeon, Parker attempts to cover the spectrum of homiletics, from personal piety to the appropriate uses of illustration.*

━━━ ━━ ━━━

Be *earnest*; be *natural*; be *as unlike a book as possible*—that is about all I have to say upon the science of homiletics. These are only heads, however; and, after the manner of preachers, you will look for a little expansion.

* Joseph Parker, *Ad Clerum: Advices to a Young Preacher* (Boston: Roberts Brothers, 1871), pp. 10-21.

As to the first head, it is happily unnecessary in your case that anything should be said merely in the way of exhortation. Your young heart glows with love to Jesus Christ, and with many a vow you have committed yourself to the holy work of publishing His name. This is the best of all beginnings. If you had begun elsewhere, you would have accomplished a swift journey to a failure as mischievous to others as it would have been humiliating to yourself. Your earnestness is my chief joy. The Cross is the strength of your heart, as it is to be the theme of your ministry; it is, you say, increasingly the solution of the mystery of life; it comes to your aid as an interpreter of all sorrow, and gives you views of sin which stir you with irrepressible desire to warn men to flee from the wrath to come. The manner in which you speak of the Cross is, to my own mind, the best assurance of the success which awaits your ministry; your apostolic enthusiasm shall not be wanting in apostolic results; he who uplifts the Cross shall surely share the exaltation and blessedness of his Lord. This holy earnestness will affect for good your entire relation to the life and service of the sanctuary, making you covetous of time, impatient of all trifling, sincere in sympathy, at once dauntless and tender in the exposition of truth, a watchful servant, and a brave soldier. There are men who unhappily imagine that it is necessary to be fussy in order to be earnest, and who wear a label on which is written, in colored letters, "This is an earnest man!" When a man is really earnest, he needs no label; he is living epistle; his whole life is his commendation. The most earnest men whom I have ever known, whether in business or in the ministry, have made their earnestness *felt* rather than *heard*; to be within the circle of their influence was to know that there was going out of them a constant and heavy expenditure of life, and that all their powers were steadfastly set in one unchanging direction. They have made this *felt*, not by the production of diaries or memoranda of service and engagement, but by an influence at once penetrating and inexplicable. It is very remarkable, too, that such men have been able to secure a tranquility which has led heedless observers to infer that they were but little in earnest about anything,—they were so quiet, so methodical, so unhurried! On the other hand, there have been fussy and effusive men who have acquired a great reputation for earnestness, when they should justly have had a name for making a great noise and a great dust. Such men have generally lost themselves in petty details; they have no clear plan, no broad and far-reaching lines of movement; their programme is made up of hop, skip, and jump, whimsically varied with jump, skip, and hop; you will have no difficulty in identifying the men when you have to suffer from the noise and the dust in which their shallow lives are wasted, but you may have a momentary difficulty in clearing your way of their vexatious intrusion. The fact that there is a spurious as well as a genuine enthusiasm leads me to detain you with a few remarks, not so much upon earnestness itself, as upon three methods of it with which you ought to be familiar: these three methods may be described as the Dental, the Porous, and the Cordial.

The *Dental* method of earnestness goes a long way with people who keep their eyes shut. The Rev. Mr. Osted was an eminent example of this method some twenty years ago. That active and most garrulous man never, to the best of my belief, spoke one word from his heart; and this is saying a good deal, for the words which he spoke were as the sand upon the seashore, innumerable. He could have preached four times not only on Sunday, but on every day of the week; and could have visited all sorts of people between the services, without so much, as drivers say, as having one turned hair. Never a word came from beyond his teeth. With a scrupulous equity worthy of a better cause, Mr. Osted spoke in the same key whether at a wedding or a funeral, and with an impartiality truly severe accosted age and infancy with the same monotonous civility. Words! why, sir, they never failed; when the apostle said "whether there be tongues they shall cease," he did not know that Mr. Osted was among the blessings of the future, though he might have suspected this fact when he predicted that "knowledge shall vanish away." You have seen a hailstorm. Yes, but no hailstorm was ever a match for Mr. Osted's tongue; and yet never a word came from beyond his teeth! I have seen him in a sick room every day for a month, but never a word came from his heart,—all dental, dental, dental! Whilst he was addressing the patient, his dry and eager eyes would be examining everything in the room, and the sweetest, tenderest words of all God's promises would almost stiffen on his freezing lips; in fact, they ceased to be promises, and became mere expressions, without unction or emphasis. Often have I turned from him with ill-disguised detestation; yet the attendant ladies, having listened to his insipid commonplaces, have blessed him for his earnestness, and said to me in his absence, "He is such a *good* man; he comes every day, wet or fine." My enforced silence under such circumstances was excellent self-discipline. . . .

Now, sir, this is the dental method of earnestness; and I need hardly add that you ought to be on your guard against it. Suspect the men who practise this method, and avoid them! They will make a tool of you; they will conduct experiments with you; and if you go too near the fire they will let you drop in, and then turn upòn their heel as if they had always thought you a fool. My heart aches when I think of the possibility of warm-hearted young ministers falling under the influence of such men. They are quite without nobility of feeling, they can say the brotherly word without the brotherly trust, their civility is as measured as if it were determined by Act of Parliament, and their patronage would be intolerable but for the condescension which is so overdone as to render itself both harmless and laughable. I have had much to do with such men. Having leaned upon them, I know them as broken staves; having watched them in the storm, I know with what ease they can set themselves to the wind; and having carefully examined their work, I can assure you it is not pleasant to look below the surface. Once for all, I repeat, suspect and avoid the Dental method of earnestness.

The *Porous* method is not illustrated so frequently now as it was a quarter of a century since, though a few very conspicuous examples occur to me at this moment,—examples of living and accountable persons, whose enthusiasm is simply a question of porousness. My fancy turns at once to a very ponderous brother, whose voice is like a clap of thunder, and whose vast bodily amplification has caused some one to say descriptively, that "he carries all before him." For the sake of easy reference, I shall call him Mr. Bodens. The manner in which that earnest gentleman exhausts himself in the pulpit is little short of alarming. No ploughman ever gasped as he gasps; no iron-founder ever sweltered at his furnace as Mr. Bodens swelters in the pulpit. His eloquence is a continual attempt at suicide, and his climaxes constantly suggest the possibility of a coroner's inquest. You will understand this when I tell you that his introduction always brings out handkerchief number one; his first head never fails to cover his face with the most varied streaks, which handkerchief number two vainly attempts to remove; the first subdivision under the second head brings on a style of breathing which can be accounted for only by internal agonies of the extremest poignancy; and the "one word more in conclusion," which always comes in immediately before "finally," drops in faint accent from a man whose earnestness has reduced him to a state of semi-liquefaction. His repute for earnestness is very high. He is spoken of by the gentler members of his congregation as "never sparing himself," "extremely energetic," "deeply devoted," and so forth. "Poor man," they say, "he does labor so when he

preaches"; "dear man, he never seems to consider *himself*, he quite
wrestles with his hearers, he is so *very earnest*"; and all this they
say with sincere esteem for Mr. Bodens and his preaching. I have
heard it again and again, and answered with a most ambiguous
sigh. From this description you will infer that Mr. Bodens is a
hard-working man, but I am bound to deny the generous inference.
There is not a stroke of hard work in him. To begin with, you cannot call him a hard reader; for beyond a few volumes of
"skeletons," he has no library; you cannot call him a hard student,
for he has often said that he never "meditates" but when in bed;
and how far he is capable of meditating there you may judge from
the fact that in his opinion "steaks and oysters are a supper for a
king," and that he enjoys the said supper as often as his funds will
allow. But though Mr. Bodens is neither a hard reader nor a hard
student, there is a sense in which he does a good deal of work, and
this ought in bare justice to be distinctly pointed out. As one of his
congregation once observed to me in a tone of much satisfaction,
"Mr. Bodens, you see, sir, is always *on the move*"; the good man
evidently thought that to be "always on the move" was the perfec-
tion of industry, and that silent contemplation was "a sort of
thing," a lucid theory which had a remarkably soothing effect
upon his own active mind. I was struck with the theory so very for-
cibly that I made it the beginning of a conversation.

"I am told, Mr. Bodens," said I, "that you are always on the
move?" I purposely heightened the last word so as to throw the re-
port into an interrogative form.

"Why, you see, sir," he replied, rounding himself to his full com-
pass, and speaking with instantaneous emotion, "my forte, I may
say without boasting, is calling upon the flock."

"You *like* it?" I replied, in a light questioning tone.

"I look upon it, sir, as one may say, in the light of duty combined
with pleasure."

"That's it, is it?" said I, without committing myself to any particular opinion.

"It *is*, sir, it *is*. You see, my brother," Mr. Bodens continued, in
the style of a lecturer on homiletics, "it helps the preaching, it
makes my discourses practical and useful."

"Don't see it," said I.

"Don't see it, sir? Why, the thing is patent, sir, quite patent; how
can you help seeing it?"

"*Prove* it," said I, quite in a challenging manner.

"Prove it? Ah, my dear sir, no young minister would have said that at the time when I began my ministry, and that will be five and thirty years ago next midsummer; my old professor always told me to visit the flock, and I should be sure to succeed in my work."

"Come now, Mr. Bodens," said I, "tell me plainly what good all this visiting does."

"Good? Why, sir, look how it promotes a happy union between the pastor and his flock!"

"Then do you mean to say that your people like that sort of thing?" I inquired.

At this point Mr. Bodens took from his pocket handkerchief number one, and then replied, "Sort of thing, sir? what sort of thing are you talking about."

"Why, visiting," said I; "do you seriously say that your people like it?"

"I say more than that, sir," Mr. Bodens haughtily replied, drawing handkerchief number one across his pudgy and wrinkled brow; "I say, sir, that they not only like it, they positively *demand* it." Mr. Bodens pronounced the word "demand," as if it involved a subpoena, and then looked at me with a steady and piercing eye.

Not wishing to go too far with the old gentleman, and observing already a faint foreshadowing of the streaks which accompany the demonstration of his first head, I fell into a conciliatory and appreciative tone, which quite pleased him.

"I should infer, then," said I, with winning blandness, "that you have a hospitable people?"

This was the right word; you should have seen the glitter of his half-buried eye! He turned round, as if to assure himself that we were alone, and then laying his hand upon my shoulder, he said, impressively,—"Brother, they *are!*"

I nodded vehemently, as if I had received an ample explanation.

"Hospitable?" Mr. Bodens continued, without changing his attitude, "can you take a word in confidence? In confidence as between brother and brother, or, as one may say, between father and son?" He then retired a pace, as if to see how that idea affected me generally.

"No doubt of it," said I, "provided it is nothing very alarming, and provided the vow is not binding after your death."

"Then," said he, "look here: just by way of curiosity I kept a memorandum of one week's hospitality; now read *that*, if you wish to know the terms upon which I live with my dear people."

"Will you read it, sir, as I am not good at making out other people's writing?"

Mr. Bodens read. There was unction in Mr. Bodens' voice; there was light in Mr. Bodens' eye; in one word, Mr. Bodens was *himself*. I quote the memorandum:—

"*Monday:* dined at H.'s; everything in season was on the table; opened a new lot of white wine. *Tuesday:* tea and supper at B.'s; a splendid game pie to supper, that would not cost a penny less than three pounds; Mrs. B. had set aside a few prime Whitstables for my special benefit, a kind creature. *Wednesday:* lunched with F., who insisted upon opening a small barrel of natives; F. is very unselfish and amusing, and would insist upon my having an extra dozen in honor of an event which had taken place in his house on the previous day. *Thursday:* paid eight visits, and supped with D. at the club; D. is a liberal friend, nothing cold would do for him, everything was steaming hot. *Friday:* took an early dinner in the Park; the table was quite a picture; a finer display of choice meats I never saw. *Saturday*, of course," Mr. Bodens added, "was spent at home."

"Well," said I, "there's no sign of famine in your note-book."

"What's the consequence?" said Mr. Bodens, as if about to establish a moral.

"Probably *bursting*," I replied, suggestively.

Mr. Bodens was shocked at this levity; he evidently regarded it as quite out of season. That earnest man never laughed. Life was too serious a business with him to admit of any pleasantry, however mild its form. Under the influence of my flippant answer, he turned himself quite round, so as to give me a complete view of his magnificent back, and personal inspection enables me to say authoritatively that in all respects it was worthy of the memorandum-book. I felt the force of the reproof, or rather I saw it; to have *felt* it would have been death upon the spot.

"Pardon me," said I, "it was quite a slip of the tongue; tell me what the consequence really is."

Mr. Bodens looked at me with much doubtfulness, as if unable to forgive the hard-hearted suggestion all at once.

"Seriously," I continued, "I wish to know the consequence."

"Consequence is, sir, according to the old proverb, a house-going minister makes a church-going people; and I can prove that to be the case, for there is not a seat in all our chapel to be let, not one, sir, even if the king himself wanted it!"

"But, Mr. Bodens, if you will excuse me, may I ask when you find time to study?"

"Study, sir?" he replied,"who wants so much study? Study your people, say I; go amongst them as a shepherd among the flock;

study their ways; make yourself acquainted with their wants; and
you can easily write out a skeleton or two on Saturday night."

"Is it right, then," I inquired, "to eat so many fat things, and to
pay for them with a skeleton?"

That was a fatal imprudence on my part. Mr. Bodens gave me a
stern and devouring look, and went away as rapidly as so vast a
personage could move. I watched his conspicuous figure until it
was out of sight, and that, as you may suppose, was a considerable
part of a lifetime. You will not wonder after this that Mr. Bodens
liquefied a good deal in his preaching, nor will you readily believe
that he perished as a martyr to the cause. Last of all, however, Mr.
Bodens died also, died of the memorandum-book. To the very end
he was spoken of as an earnest preacher, and even to this day there
are old members of his congregation who reverently recall the occasions when Mr. Bodens was so exhausted with preaching as
hardly to be able to get into the vestry in the customary manner of
solid bodies. When he died he left a great blank.

By the *Cordial* method of earnestness is meant, of course, the
method of the heart. We must be earnest as *Christians*, before we
can be earnest as *ministers*. How can our work be right if our heart
be wrong? And how can our heart be made right but by constant
watching at the Cross? Though we are ministers of Jesus Christ, yet
we are poor sinners; our salvation is not in ourselves, but in the Son
of God; and if for a moment we imagine that our ministry involves
an exemption from the lowliness and contrition which become
guilty men, we fall from grace, and our strength is withered. When
we come from the Cross heart-broken, and yet glad in the salvation
which has been wrought for us, our words will be simple, our manners will be natural, and our tone will be none the less persuasive
because it falters with the emotion of thankfulness for our redemption. Truly, our weakness is our strength; when we feel our own
nothingness, the grace of Christ is most magnified in our hearts;
and when the shallow channel of our invented eloquence is quite
dry, God gives us His word as a well of water whose springs never
fail. Out of this earnestness will come a simplicity which cannot be
understood, a candor which is above suspicion, and an independence as superior to flattery as it is scornful of intimidation.
"Keep thy heart with all diligence, for out of it are the issues of
life." To fail there, is to fail altogether! "Take heed to thyself, and
keep thy soul diligently, lest thou forget the things which thine eyes
have seen, and lest they depart from thy heart all the days of thy
life." See how we are thus urged to personal consecration! What is

our standing before God? Is our love deep as our life, or is it but a transient impulse? Is Jesus Christ merely a theme to be talked about, or is He the strength of our heart and our portion forever? Is our Christian experience a luxury with which we pamper our self-ishness, or does it constrain us to abundant service such as no hireling would ever undertake? These are questions which call us into the secrecy and terribleness of Divine judgment.

3

John Henry Jowett
1864-1923

John Henry Jowett was as dedicated to preaching as a man could be. Perhaps that is why he served only large churches. Most of us progress to larger churches as we improve and mature as preachers and pastors. The first church which Jowett pastored was Carr's Lane Congregational Church, Birmingham, England. The auditorium of Carr's Lane seated more than one thousand persons. It was regularly filled to hear Jowett's preaching. Jowett served Carr's Lane from 1895 to 1911. He pastored Fifth Avenue Presbyterian Church, New York City, until 1918 when he returned to war-torn London as pastor of Westminster Chapel.

*The secret of Jowett's success can be largely attributed to hard work. In the following excerpt Jowett describes the arduous preparation which he felt every preacher should make before entering the pulpit. The excerpt, which is from chapter four of **The Preacher: His Life and Work,** is entitled "The Preacher in His Study."** *

I am to-day to ask your consideration to the subject of "The Preacher in His Study." What manner of man must the preacher be when he enters his workshop, and what kind of work shall he do? A little while ago I was reading the life of a very distinguished Eng-

* John H. Jowett, *The Preacher: His Life and Work* (1912; reprint ed., Grand Rapids: Baker Book House, 1968), pp. 113-41.

lish judge, Lord Bowen, and in an illuminating statement of the powers and qualities required for success at the bar he used these words: "Cases are won in chambers." That is to say, so far as the barrister is concerned, his critical arena is not the public court but his own private room. He will not win triumph by extemporary wit, but by hard work. Cases are not won by jaunty "sorties" of flashing appeal, but by well-marshalled facts and disciplined arguments marching solidly together in invincible strength. "Cases are won in chambers." And if a barrister is to practically conquer his jury before he meets them, by the victorious strength and sway of his preparations, shall it be otherwise with a preacher, before he seeks the verdict of his congregation? With us, too, "cases are won in chambers." Men are not deeply influenced by extemporized thought. They are not carried along by a current of fluency which is ignorant where it is going. Mere talkativeness will not put people into bonds. Happy-go-lucky sermons will lay strong constraint upon the heart. Preaching that costs nothing accomplishes nothing. If the study is a lounge the pulpit will be an impertinence.

It is, therefore, imperative that the preacher go into his study to do hard work. We must make the business-man in our congregation feel that we are his peer in labour. There is no man so speedily discovered as an idle minister, and there is no man who is visited by swifter contempt. We may hide some things, but our idleness is as obtrusive as though the name of sluggard were branded on our foreheads. As indeed it is! . . . If we have no system we shall come to think we were working when we were only thinking about it, and that we were busy when we were only engaged. And, therefore, with all my heart I give this counsel,—be as systematic as a business-man. Enter your study at an appointed hour, and let that hour be as early as the earliest of your business-men goes to his warehouse or his office . . . Let first things be put first, and let him give the freshness of his strength to matters of vital and primary concern. Gentlemen, all this will pay, and the payment will be made in sterling good. You will win the respect of your people, even of the most strenuous of them, and when they see that you "mean business" some of your obstacles will be already removed, and you will find an open way to the very citadels of their souls . . . .

. . . I would, therefore, urge upon all young preachers, amid all their other reading, to be always engaged in the comprehensive study of some one book in the Bible. Let that book be studied with all the strenuous mental habits of a man's student days. Let him put into it the deliberate diligence, the painstaking care, the steady persistence with which he prepared for exacting examinations, and let him assign a part of every day to attaining perfect mastery over it. You will find this habit to be of immeasurable value in the enrichment of your ministry. In the first place, it will give you breadth of vision, and, therefore, it will give you perspective and proportion. You will see every text as coloured and determined by its context, and indeed as related to vast provinces of truth which might otherwise seem remote and irrelevant. And you will be continually fertilizing your minds by discoveries and surprises which will keep you from boredom, and which will keep you from that wearisome gin of commonplaces in whose accustomed grooves even the most stalwart grows faint. Wide journeyings and explorations of this kind will leave you no trouble about texts. Texts will clamour for recognition, and your only trouble will be to find time to give them notice. The year will seem altogether too short to deal with the waiting procession and to exhibit their wealth. Yes, you will be embarrassed with your riches instead of with your poverty . . . .

In your study you will, of course, take advantage of the best that scholarship can offer you in the interpretation of the Word. Before preaching upon any passage you will make the most patient inquisition, and under the guidance of acknowledged masters you will seek to realize the precise conditions in which the words were born. And here I want most strongly to urge you to cultivate the power of historical imagination: I mean the power to reconstitute the dead realms of the past and to repeople them with moving life . . . Many of us have only a partial power, and it leaves us with maimed interpretations. To a certain extent we can refashion the past, but it is like Pompeii, it is dead. We get a setting, but not the life. Things are not in movement. We cannot transpose ourselves back with all our senses, and see things in all their play and interplay, and catch the sounds and secrets in the air, and touch the hurrying people in the streets, or nod to the shepherd on the hills. We may see the past as a photograph: we do not see it as a cinematograph. Things are not alive! And to see men alive is by no means an easy attainment. We cannot get it by reverie: it is the fruit of firm, steady, illumined imagination.

How are we to preach about Amos unless we can live with him on the hills of Tekoa, and see his environment as if it were part of our own surroundings, every sense active in its own reception: and unless we can go with him into Bethel, and note the very things that he sees along the road, and see the moving, tainted, insincere and rotten life which is congested in the town? How can we enter into the teaching of the Prophet Hosea unless by the power of a vividly exercised imagination we recover his surroundings? The Book of Hosea is filled with sights and sounds and scents. We must go back to his day and all our senses must be as open channels to the impressions that appealed to him. We must go with him along the streets, we must look into the houses and workshops. We must see the baker at his oven and kings and princes in their palace. We must walk with him through the lanes and among the fields at dawn of day when "the morning cloud" is beginning to lift and the grass is drenched with "the early dew." We must see Hosea's homeland if we would intimately appreciate his speech. . . .

I am urging the cultivation of the historical imagination because I am persuaded that the want of it so often gives unreality to our preaching. If we do not realize the past we cannot get its vital message for the present. The past which is unfolded in the pages of Scripture is to many of us very wooden: and the men and the women are wooden: we do not feel their breathing: we do not hear them cry: we do not hear them laugh: we do not mix with their humanness and find that they are just like folk in the next street. And so the message is not alive. It does not pulse with actuality. It is too often a dead word belonging to a dead world, and it has no gripping relevancy to the throbbing lives of our own day. And so I urge you to cultivate the latent power of realization, the power to fill with breath the motionless forms of the past. If needful, before you preach upon an old-world message, spend a whole morning in hard endeavour to recall and vitalize the old world, until it becomes so vivid that you can scarcely tell whether you are a preacher in your study, or a citizen in some village, or city, or empire of the past. . . .

. . . Now it is a good thing to put a subject away to mature and clarify. When my grandmother was making cider she used to let it stand for long seasons in the sunlight "to give it a soul!" And I think that many of our sermons, when the preliminary work has been done, should be laid aside for a while, before they are offered to our congregations. There are subconscious powers in the life that seem to continue the ripening process when our active judgments are engaged elsewhere. The subject "gets a soul," the sediment settles down, and in its lucidity it becomes like "the river of water of life, clear as crystal." Every preacher of experience will tell you that he has some sermons that have been "standing in the sun" for years, slowly maturing, and clarifying, but not yet ready to offer to the people. One of my congregation in Birmingham once asked Dr.

Dale to preach upon a certain text in the epistle to the Romans, and he said he would seriously think about it. Long afterwards she reminded him of his promise, and she asked him when the sermon was coming. Dr. Dale answered her with great seriousness, "It is not ready yet!" At another time he was asked by another of his people to preach a course of sermons on some of the great evangelical chapters in the book of the prophecies of Isaiah. He made the same reply, "I am not ready yet." I came upon a similar instance in the life of Beecher. He was to preach at an ordination service in New England. He said to Dr. Lyman Abbott, "I think I shall preach a sermon on pulpit dynamics; you had better look out for it." "I did look for it," continued Dr. Abbott, "and it was nothing but a description of the incidental advantages of the ministry as a profession. When I next met Beecher I asked, 'Where is that sermon on pulpit dynamics?' 'It was not ripe,' he replied."

The weakness of smaller preachers is that their time is "always ready": the mighty preachers have long seasons when they know their time "is not yet come." They have the strength to go slowly and even to "stand." They do not "rush into print," or into speech, with "unproportioned thought." They can keep the message back, sometimes for years, until some day there is a soul in it, and a movement about it, which tells them "the hour is come." Beware of the facility which, if given a day's notice, is ready to preach on anything! Let us cultivate the strength of leisureliness, the long, strong processes of meditation, the self-control that refuses to be premature, the discipline that can patiently await maturity. "Let patience have her perfect work."

I have a conviction that no sermon is ready for preaching, not ready for writing out, until we can express its theme in a short, pregnant sentence as clear as a crystal. I find the getting of that sentence is the hardest, the most exacting, and the most fruitful labour in my study. To compel oneself to fashion that sentence, to dismiss every word that is vague, ragged, ambiguous, to think oneself through to a form of words which defines the theme with scrupulous exactness,—this is surely one of the most vital and essential factors in the making of a sermon: and I do not think any sermon ought to be preached or even written, until that sentence has emerged, clear and lucid as a cloudless moon. Do not confuse obscurity with profundity, and do not imagine that lucidity is necessarily shallow. Let the preacher bind himself to the pursuit of clear conceptions, and let him aid his pursuit by demanding that every sermon he preaches shall express its theme and purpose in a sentence as lucid as his powers can command. All this will mean that the preparation of Sunday's sermons cannot begin on Saturday morning and finish on Saturday night. The preparation is a long process: the best sermons are not made, they grow: they have their analogies, not in the manufactory, but in the garden and the field.

I need not, perhaps, say that in all the leisurely preparation of a sermon we must keep in constant and immediate relation to life. The sermon is not to be a disquisition on abstract truth, some clever statement of unapplied philosophy, some brilliant handling of remote metaphysics. The sermon must be a proclamation of truth as vitally related to living men and women. It must *touch* life where the touch is significant, both in its crises and its commonplaces. It must be truth that travels closely with men, up hill, down hill, or over the monotonous plain. And, therefore, the preacher's message must first of all "touch" the preacher himself. It must be truth that "finds" him in his daily life, truth that lies squarely upon his own circumstances, that fits his necessities, that fills the gaps of his needs as the inflowing tide fills the bays and coves along the shore. If the truth he preaches has no urgent relation to himself, if it does no business down his road, if it offers no close and serious fellowship in his journeyings, the sermon had best be laid aside. But the truth of a sermon must also make recognition of lives more varied than our own, and in the preparation of our sermons these must be kept in mind. I know that God "hath fashioned their hearts alike," and that the fundamental needs of men are everywhere the same: and yet there are great differences in temperament, and vast varieties of circumstances, of which we have to take account if our message is to find entry into new lives, and to have both attraction and authority. Perhaps you will permit me to illustrate by mentioning my own plan. When I have got my theme clearly defined, and I begin to prepare its exposition, I keep in the circle of my mind at least a dozen men and women, very varied in their natural temperaments, and very dissimilar in their daily circumstances. These are not mere abstractions. Neither are they dolls or dummies. They are real men and women whom I know: professional people, trading people, learned and ignorant, rich and poor. When I am preparing my work, my mind is constantly glancing round this invisible circle, and I consider how I can so serve the bread of this particular truth as to provide welcome nutriment for all. What relation has this teaching to that barrister? How can the truth be related to that doctor? What have I here for that keenly nervous man with the artistic temperament? And there is that poor body upon whom the floods of sorrow have been rolling their billows for many years—what about her? And so on all round the circle. You may not like my method: it probably would not suit you, and you may devise a better: but at any rate it does this for me,—in all my preparation it keeps me in actual touch with life, with real men and women, moving in the common streets, exposed to life's varying weathers, the "garish day," and the cold night, the gentle dew and the driving blast. It keeps me on the common earth: it saves me from losing myself in the clouds. Gentlemen, our messages must be related to life, to lives, and we must make everybody feel that our key fits the lock of his own private door.

With our purpose thus clearly defined, and keeping sight of actual men and women, we shall arrange our thought and message accordingly. There will be one straight road of exposition, making directly for the enlightenment of the mind, leading on to the capture of the judgment, on to the rousing of the conscience, on to the conquest of the will. This last sentence used figures of speech that are significant of military tactics, and we do, indeed, require something of military strategy, in its vigilance and ingenuity, in seeking to win Mansoul for the Lord. How to so expound and arrange the truth, along what particular ways to direct it, so as to change foes into allies and enlarge the bounds of the Kingdom of Christ,—that is the problem that confronts the preacher every time he prepares his sermon. And it may be, it probably will be, that you will reject outline after outline, outline after outline, discarding them all as too indefinite and uncertain, until one is planned which seems to lead undeviatingly to the much-desired end. First get your bare straight road, with a clear issue: go no further until that road is made: later on you may open springs of refreshment, and you may have even flowers and bird-song along the way. But, first of all, I say, "Prepare ye the way of the people: cast up, cast up the highway: gather out the stones."

When all the preliminary labour is finished, and you begin to write your message, let me advise you not to be the bondslave to much-worn phraseology, and to forms of expression which have ceased to be significant. I do not counsel you to be unduly aggressive, and still less, irreverent, in your treatment of old terminology, but you will find amazing power in the newness of carefully chosen expressions, offered as new vehicles of old truth. A famous doctor told me that sickly people are often helped in their appetites by a frequent change of the ware on which their food is served. The new ware gives a certain freshness to the accustomed food. And so it is in the ministry of the word. A "new way of putting a thing" awakens zest and interest where the customary expression might leave the hearer listless and indifferent.

And in this matter of expression let me add one further word. Do not foolishly attach value to carelessness and disorder. Pay sacred heed to the ministry of style. When you have discovered a jewel give it the most appropriate setting. When you have discovered a truth give it the noblest expression you can find. A fine thought can bear, indeed it demands, a fine expression. A well-ordered, well-shaped sentence, carrying a body and weight of truth, will strangely influence even the uncultured hearer. We make a fatal mistake if we assume that uncultivated people love the uncouth. I have heard Henry Drummond address a meeting of "waifs and strays," a sombre little company of ragged, neglected, Edinburgh youngsters, and he spake to them with a simplicity and a finished refinement which added the spell of beauty to the vigour of the truth. There was no luxuriance, no flowery rhetoric: nothing of that sort: but the style was the servant of that truth, and, whether he was giving warning or encouragement, making them laugh or making them wonder, the sentences were "gentlemanly," a combination of beauty and strength.

And as for the illustrations we may use in our exposition of a truth I have only one word to say. An illustration that requires explanation is worthless. A lamp should do its own work. I have seen illustrations that were like pretty drawing-room lamps, calling attention to themselves. A real preacher's illustrations are like street lamps, scarcely noticed, but throwing floods of light upon the road. Ornamental lamps will be of little or no use to you: honest street-lamps will serve your purpose at every turning.

4

Andrew Blackwood
1882-1966

Andrew Blackwood was a pastor and a teacher before filling the chair of Practical Theology at Princeton University in 1930. One of his goals in life was to put homiletics on the academic map. In the midst of the theological controversies then embroiling Princeton, Blackwood introduced several innovations in the teaching of homiletics. He introduced courses in audience psychology and practicum and lab situations in his teaching. He also began a prolific career as an author of books on homiletics while at Princeton. In 1950 he became Professor of Homiletics at the Temple University School of Theology, where he concluded his teaching career in 1958.

*The following excerpt is from chapter six of Blackwood's book, **The Preparation of Sermons**. The chapter title is "The Marks of Effective Style."** *

The writing of sermons calls for the skill of an artist in the use of words. At one and the same time he can set forth life and motion, warmth and color, beauty and force. All of that, under God, depends on a man's personality, and personality ever eludes our grasp, like quicksilver. But now we turn to something tangible. Not every young minister knows how to prepare a discourse with all of

* Andrew Blackwood, *The Preparation of Sermons* (Nashville: Abingdon Press, 1958), pp. 183-92.

these excellences, certainly not once or twice a week; but every young preacher can form the habit of testing his handiwork, and striving to make it better week after week. So let him take as a motto the words of Paul to young Timothy: "Do your best to present yourself to God as one approved, a workman who has no need to be ashamed, rightly handling the word of truth" (II Tim. 2:15 RSV).

How then should a minister judge his written work? Let us bring the matter down to earth and out into the open. Here lies a manuscript after the first writing. Let us begin with the simplest and easiest test, that of clarity. Clarity refers to writing and speaking that no reader or hearer can misunderstand. Only a visitor among churches can know how many intelligent laymen fail to follow the pastor's sermons. In recent days such complaints have come to one observer from lay officers in churches far from each other and far from his home. In reporting about a pastor with ability, these laymen complain, "Half the time some of us do not know what he is driving at, and we wonder if he knows!"

In his autobiography Joseph Fort Newton quotes the president of a large university:

> That is the first sermon I have heard in a long time that I understood. Men have come here to argue about God, trying to prove something that nobody denies until they try to prove it. As a layman I am not up on theology, but you talked about life.

Perhaps those visiting preachers strove to seem scholarly, but if so, they did not know how, and they merely stirred up waters full of mud. In the same book Newton tells how he first sensed the importance of making everything clear to the average man or woman. He concludes that clarity calls for far more ability and work than its opposite.

Among ordinary churchgoers, a gloomy observer estimates that about 2 per cent of the preaching gets across. Now that psychologists have begun to test the "audience response" in church, some of them would raise the proportion a little, but not far. They would also advise the pastor to sit down in his study and test his written work. How? The answer may come from a recent book by an expert in his field, Rudolf Flesch, whose work has nothing directly to do with religion. This author ignores the beauty of written words, and goes into mathematical calculations that do not concern us here. Otherwise his principles will guide any clergyman in checking up on his preaching style.

If a minister wishes to make everything in a sermon clear, he must feel sure about the goal, and then have a sense of direction. He must school himself to state and explain, describe and discuss. At times he must repeat, and perhaps illustrate. For examples of such clarity turn to Macaulay, in whose prose works clear writing comes from clear thinking. On the other hand, alas, clear thinking does not always lead to clear writing and speaking. Hence a minister needs to revise the first draft of his sermon.

Revision may begin with the paragraph. In modern prose a writer or speaker who knows his business pays attention to the paragraph, giving it much the same treatment that the composer of a hymn accords the stanza. Current practice calls for paragraphs of about a hundred words, perhaps a little more. If the units of thought run much over a hundred words, the work may seem heavy. If the paragraphs stop short of a hundred words, the effect may become choppy. Within the limits of a hundred words, or a little more, a writer or speaker can state and develop a single idea. If he wishes to say more, he can frame another paragraph. All of this may sound like machine work, but so would any statement about the length of stanzas in a hymn.

Each paragraph may start with a key sentence, clear and crisp. The rest of the hundred words explain and enforce the idea in the opening sentence. After the final revision, when the preacher goes over the manuscript before the hour of delivery, he can size it up by glancing at the key sentences. If he expects to preach from notes, he can write down the paragraph openings; and if he wishes fuller notes, he can jot down both the beginning and the end of each unit. A good paragraph starts with clarity and ends with force. All that comes between the first sentence and the last one helps to round out the whole. For an example of such a paragraph read aloud Lincoln's address at Gettysburg. Better still, divide it into two parts, each with a few more than a hundred words.

Within the paragraph look at the sentences. Are they clear and easy to follow? Does the same subject carry over from sentence to sentence, or does the thought shift back and forth like a tennis ball in a championship match? Does the same tense prevail, or must the attention turn from past to present and from future to past? How often does the speaker expect the hearer to shift his mental gears? As often as necessary to follow the thought, but a wise speaker learns to avoid shifting within a paragraph. Of course someone might apply these suggestions crudely, as with a hammer. But if a man works carefully, as an artist toils over a painting before he counts it complete, the paragraphs and sentences will come out clear.

In each paragraph the final sentence ought to prepare for what follows. In the next paragraph the opening sentence should tie up with what has gone before. Then the successive parts will constitute a train of thought, with never a break from the beginning to the end of the sermon. Such writing and speaking calls for the use of connectives, all sorts of connectives except the conspicuous. As coupling pins these words and phrases show transitions from paragraph to paragraph, and often from sentence to sentence. Coupling pins appear more often in the work of a teaching minister than in that of an inspirational speaker. For instance, you find more careful use of connectives in the sermons of Bushnell than in those of Brooks, in the pulpit work of Fosdick than in the pep talks of "Dr. Sunny Jim."

As for sentences, no young minister would try to carry out all of the following suggestions in one week. But in the course of months a few rules may help a man secure clarity.

1. *Avoid making a detour* within a sentence. Keep on the main highway. Never clutter up a sentence with a parenthesis, like the one that follows, in the sort of sloppy stuff that some of us think profound: "In writing a treatise a scholarly author (knowing that the reader can glance back and see where he got off the road) may—like a playwright in an 'aside'—employ parentheses such as these, but twice as long and much more tortuous."

2. *Keep the subject close to the predicate.* As a minister grows older, he tends to introduce explanatory clauses, and so to become increasingly incoherent. When he comes to the middle of a sentence that rambles over the hills like a rail fence, he forgets where that section of the fence ought to end. If any reader feels that he has learned how to keep from rambling, let him secure a recording machine and have an expert take down the sermon and the prayers next Sunday morning. Only an exceptional leader goes through an hour of public worship without using sentences that wobble or break down in the middle.

3. *Keep most of the sentences short.* In the words of Flaubert, a master of the novel, "Banish the semicolon. Whenever you can shorten the sentence, do. And one always can. The best sentence? The shortest!" In the handiwork of a dunce the habit of using short sentences might lead to nonsense or even bathos, but why should a dunce try to preach? Even if a dunce did preach, he would not write out sermons and then revise them with care. Only a wise man

does that. But not every wise man keeps his sentences short. Gossip feels free at times to use ones that run beyond a hundred words, whereas Flesch recommends an average of about seventeen. The best wisdom of our day calls for prose sentences shorter than those of yesterday, but still not choppy.

4. Within the sentence *watch the sequence of ideas* by keeping your eye on the ball. Avoid saying, "When the people assembled for worship, a beautiful Cross was seen." Fix attention on the people, or else on the Cross. Form the habit of using an active verb to show action: "When the people gathered for worship, they beheld a beautiful Cross." This habit of keeping the mind moving in the same direction may help a man to avoid embarrassment. In the copy for next Sunday morning's bulletin he may have to correct an item from the church secretary: "At the Women's Society last Thursday, Miss Minerva Brown spoke on 'Personal Devils'; sixty-five were present."

The Call for Interest

We might go on to think about clarity in the use of words, but we turn to human interest, only to find it more important and more difficult to attain. Needless to say, the two terms overlap, for both clarity and interest have to do with words, sentences, and paragraphs, even with whole sermons. Sometimes, however, the claims of clarity and those of interest seem to conflict. Clarity may call for short sentences, but a succession of them, too much alike, might become as monotonous as ties in a railroad track. When the use of short sentences begins to attract attention to itself, the speaker has employed one too many. In short, keep your balance!

Any child of ten can write short sentences, straight and stiff, like pickets in a fence. But a man who knows his Bible can use sentences that accord with the tone color of what he wishes to say. Often he employs something with a balance that resembles Hebrew parallelism, much as our Lord spoke about treasures on earth and treasures in heaven. Robertson preached this way, if only for variety. As an example of a balanced sentence take this one about Great Britain: "The king has glory without much power; the prime minister has power without much glory."

Robertson framed many of his sentences this way because his mind and heart dwelt much on truths that balanced. For a more recent example of a balanced style turn to part of a message by Henry Van Dyke. At a university chapel he spoke on "The Meaning of

Manhood," from the text: "How much then is a man better than a sheep?" (Matt. 12:12).

> "How much is that man worth?" asks the curious observer. "That man," says the walking business directory, "is worth a million dollars: and the man sitting next to him is not worth a penny.' . . .
>
> What can this man make; how much has that man made; how much can I make out of this man's labor; how much will that man pay for my services? . . .
>
> Those little children that play in the streets—they are nothing to me or to the world; they are worthless. Those long-fleeced, highbred sheep that feed upon my pastures—they are among my most costly possessions; they will bring an enormous price; they are immensely valuable. 'How much, then, is a man better than a sheep?' What a foolish question! Sometimes the man is better; sometimes the sheep is better. It all depends on the supply and demand.

The use of balance in sentences and elsewhere in writing calls for ability and practice. The mastery of the periodic sentence affords a still more conclusive proof of a man's education and culture. In our day, however, through no fault of his own, many a college graduate seems never to have heard of the periodic sentence. When a seminary student asks what the term means, the professor may quote an example: "Though I speak with the tongues of men and of angels, and have not love, I am become as sounding brass" (I Cor. 13:1). If the Apostle had stopped there, he would have used periodic structure, but the sentence goes on with another phrase that adds to the charm: "or a tinkling cymbal." In the verse as a whole note the alliteration and the assonance, the rhythm and the repetition for emphasis.

In reading or speaking a periodic sentence the minister needs to sustain his voice, with a sort of suspense, and not let it fall until he comes to the word that completes his thought the first time; in this case, "brass." In that message from Van Dyke the use of balanced sentences gives way at times to the periodic; for example, "If wealth is really the measure of value, if the end of life is the production or acquisition of riches, then humanity must take its place in the sliding scale of commodities." More tersely, a concert artist tells a beginner: "When you stand up to sing, if you feel nervous, slowly inhale three full breaths." In like manner, young minister, if you would add to the variety and appeal of your spoken words, learn to use a periodic sentence occasionally, if only for the sake of variety and suspense.

In that sermon from Van Dyke the closing paragraph illustrates another "rule of the road": a few successive sentences alike in form often prove more effective than an equal number of statements all diverse. In the appeal that follows note the use of parallelism, the quietness of rhythm, the repetition for emphasis, and the willingness to stop before repetition tires. Also see how Van Dyke as a pulpit master spoke to the heart of the university student:

> Come then to Christ, who alone can save you from the sin that defiles and destroys your manhood. Come then to Christ, who alone can make you good men and true, living in the power of an endless life. Come then to Christ, that you may have fellowship with Him, and realize all it means to be a man.

"All it means to be a man!" What an ending for a message about "The Meaning of Manhood"! The ability to speak with clarity and interest depends almost as much on mastery of words as of sentences. "No material with which human beings work has so much potential energy as words." Through everyday use of the dictionary, and through the companionship of books, the minister can discipline himself to speak correctly and precisely without seeming pedantic. He knows that "few" relates to number and "less" to quantity, that a farmer "sows" wheat and "plants" corn, but never feeds "fodder" to sheep. In the church bulletin and elsewhere the pastor avoids referring to "Reverend Jones" in lieu of "The Reverend John Henry Jones," "The Rev. Dr. Jones" or occasionally, "Rev. John H. Jones."

Much more important than such precision is human interest. If a preacher wishes to use words that appeal to ordinary people, let him widen the range of his vocabulary. Where a novice would employ the colorless word "great" to describe everything from a sonnet to a cyclone, Bushnell or Gossip would give the call to live words, fact words, action words, words with "hands and feet." By using live words the speaker can show the hearer a succession of motion pictures. For examples of live words go to the teachings of our Lord, especially to that parable about the two builders: "I will liken him unto a wise man, which built his house upon a rock; and the rain descended, and the floods came, and the winds blew, and beat upon that house; and it fell not: for it was founded upon a rock" (Matt. 7:24-25).

In these forty-three words note the number of appeals to see, to feel, to do. Of such live words a student has found fifteen, or one out of every three. Whatever the number, it exceeds that on many a page of sermonic prose. Once again, note how the Master Teacher heightens the effect by going on to repeat His words, this time negatively, about the house on the sand. In each half of the word picture he points to one builder, not to eight or ten, and to one in action, not in repose. The Teacher also throws His stress on nouns and verbs, especially verbs of action. Except for "wise man" and "foolish man," each of which points to a single builder, He employs no descriptive adjective or adverb. By such artistry in the use of words He attains a beauty like that of a rainbow after a storm in June.

> God wove a web of loveliness,
> Of clouds and storms and birds,
> But made not anything at all
> So beautiful as words.

By way of contrast, see how not to use words. In 1768 a New Testament "scholar," Edward Harwood, issued what he styled an "elegant rendering" of the parable we all know best and love most. In this excerpt note the scarcity of live words, and then look at the "duds." See how the use of modifiers weakens the effect in detail and mars the picture as a whole:

> A gentleman of a splendid family and opulent fortune had two sons. One day the younger approached his father, and begged him in the most importunate and soothing terms to make a partition of his effects betwixt himself and his elder brother. The indulgent father, overcome by his blandishments, immediately divided all his fortune between them.

Today no one but a pedant would resort to such pomposity. However, with a jargon all our own we of today can make the prodigal son and his brother seem commonplace or unreal. Even when we refer to the father who forgave his younger son, we may talk in terms of "reaction," "characterization," "realization," and "implications." We may overwork "particularly"—a word especially difficult to articulate. In other connections we may refer to "this war-torn world," "the far-flung battle line," and "needing no introduction to this audience." Why should an educated man ever resort to a cliche? A wise minister, though a Protestant, can set up an *Index Expurgatorius*; at least he can follow the injunction of Alexander Pope:

> In words as fashions the same rule will hold,
> Alike fantastic if too new or old;
> Be not the first by whom the new are tried,
> Nor yet the last to lay the old aside.

Fortunately no minister needs all of these counsels. If in college and seminary a young man has formed the right sort of habits, most of these matters take care of themselves. In lieu of such discipline in the past a young preacher may need to check up on his ways of using words, sentences, and paragraphs. The man whose pulpit speech tends to be clear and dull needs to discover ways of securing interest, whereas the one who knows how to grip the hearer, only to leave him confused, needs to strive after clarity. In the pulpit human interest far outweighs clearness, but still many an interesting preacher ought to study the words of our Lord: "He that received seed into good ground is he that heareth the word, and understandeth it" (Matt. 13:23).

Does any pastor wish to enjoy writing a sermon every week? If so, let him determine to prepare every message as well as his abilities permit. In the service of our King, whatever a man does well he begins to enjoy, and whatever he enjoys he tends to do well. "Learning to write may be a serious business, but it need not be a solemn one." As for ability to write with ease, and at times with a touch of distinction, all of that comes to the man who lives with good books, especially poetry, and then writes something every day—it may be a prayer. "Write much, if you would write well."

What an ideal! To transform drudgery into delight! Even if this ideal eludes a man's grasp, the pursuit will bring him satisfaction of heart. As the biographies of countless artists make clear, every man who would become a master of words must toil at his task.